ISBN 978-0-364-77505-9
PIBN 11272925

This book is a reproduction of an important historical work. Forgotten Books uses
state-of-the-art technology to digitally reconstruct the work, preserving the original format
whilst repairing imperfections present in the aged copy. In rare cases, an imperfection in
the original, such as a blemish or missing page, may be replicated in our edition. We do,
however, repair the vast majority of imperfections successfully; any imperfections that
remain are intentionally left to preserve the state of such historical works.

A SALLE COLLEGE 1974-75 BASKETBALL HANDBOOK

Table of Contents

Photography by Mark Jacobson
On The Cover: All American Candidate Bill Taylor (see page 9)

This handbook is dedicated to the members of the Press, Radio and Television corps by La Salle College's News Bureau with the cooperation of the College's Department of Athletics. For further information, please call, write or wire:

JOSEPH B. BATORY
Sports Information Director,
La Salle College News Bureau
Philadelphia, Penna. 19141
Office Phone: (Area Code 215)
VIctor 8-8300, Ext. 465
Home Phone: 609-662-0212

Limited quantity of Handbooks available to the Public at $1.00 each.

LASALLE COLLEGE

1974-75 SEASON AT A GLANCE

INSTITUTION: La Salle College

LOCATION: 20th Street and Olney Avenue, Philadelphia, Pa. 19141

TELEPHONE: (Area Code 215) 848-8300

COLLEGE FOUNDED: 1863   1974-75 ENROLLMENT: 6300

TEAM NICKNAME: Explorers   COLORS: Blue and Gold

CONFERENCE: East Coast Conference

PRESIDENT: Brother Daniel Burke, F.S.C., Ph.D.

ATHLETIC DIRECTOR: John J. Conboy (La Salle, 1950)

ASSISTANT ATHLETIC DIRECTOR: Joseph O'Donnell (La Salle, 1965)

SPORTS INFORMATION DIRECTOR: Joseph B. Batory (La Salle, 1964)

HEAD BASKETBALL COACH: Paul W. Westhead (St. Joseph's, 1961), Fifth
Year, 59-46

ASSISTANT COACHES: Joseph O'Connor (St. Joseph's, 1963); Paul Gallagher (La Salle, 1964); Dave "Lefty" Ervin (La Salle, 1968)

TEAM PHYSICIAN: Dr. Eugene Gallagher (La Salle, 1947)

ATHLETIC TRAINER: John Greer

EQUIPMENT MANAGER: Charles M. Loughran

1973-74 VARSITY RECORD: 18-10, overall; 5-1 conference (second); 2-2
Big Five (second)

KEY LETTERMEN LOST: 6-6 Joe DiCocco (10.5 ppg.-9.4 rpg.); 6-1 Steve
Baruffi (5.8 ppg.).

TOP RETURNING LETTERMEN: 6-5 Bill Taylor (19.7 ppg.-7.0 rpg.); 6-10
Joe Bryant (18.7 ppg.-10.8 rpg.); 6-0 Charlie Wise (11.9 ppg.); and 6-2
Glenn Collier (7.3 ppg.).

NEW OPPONENTS ON 1974-75 REGULAR SEASON SCHEDULE:
Memphis State

1974-75 CAPTAIN: Bill Taylor

PRONUNCIATION GUIDE

BRODZINSKI ....Brod-ZIN'-ski

WOLKIEWICZ ....Wol-KAY'-vitch

2

ATHLETIC DEPARTMENT STAFF

JOHN J. CONBOY
Athletic Director

John J. (Jack) Conboy was named La Salle athletic director on January 3, 1969, succeeding James J. Henry, who retired January 1 after 35 years as Explorer A.D.

Conboy, 48, graduated from La Salle in 1950. He recently retired from the U.S. Army with the rank of lieutenant colonel after 20 years service. A veteran of three wars (WW II, Korea and Vietnam), Conboy served on the ROTC staff at La Salle from 1960-64.

Conboy was a member of St. Joseph's Prep's last city championship football team in 1939. After three years of World War II service in Europe, Conboy enrolled at Georgetown where he played football for two years before transferring to La Salle.

He was assistant football coach at St. Joseph's Prep from 1948 to 1950. He also coached Army football and basketball teams in Europe and Hawaii and organized a triathlon team at La Salle which produced three former members of the U.S. Army modern pentathlon team— Don Walheim, Bill Conroy and Gary McNulty.

Conboy, who holds an M.B.A. degree in Industrial Management from Temple University, resides in Drexel Hill, Pa. with his wife, Anne, and four children.

JOSEPH F. O'DONNELL
Assistant Athletic Director

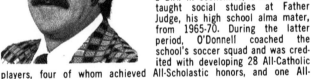

Joseph F. O'Donnell was appointed assistant A.D. and coordinator of Hayman Hall, the college's $4.0 million physical recreation center in March of 1972.

A 1965 graduate of La Salle with a B.A. in economics, O'Donnell had taught social studies at Father Judge, his high school alma mater, from 1965-70. During the latter period, O'Donnell coached the school's soccer squad and was credited with developing 28 All-Catholic players, four of whom achieved All-Scholastic honors, and one All-American status.

In 1970-71 O'Donnell moved to a full-time position with the City of Philadelphia as recreation leader at the Jardel Center. He was a member of the Department of Recreation Soccer Committee, and also assisted Bill Wilkinson with the 1970 Explorer soccer team which posted the first winning season in the college's history.

O'Donnell, 29, and his wife, Marie, reside in northeast Philadelphia.

Dr. Eugene Gallagher
Team Physician

John Greer
Trainer

Charles M. Loughran
Equipment Manager

MEET THE EXPLORER COACHING STAFF

PAUL W. WESTHEAD
Head Basketball Coach

La Salle College basketball coach Paul Westhead, 34, has rapidly established himself as one of the better young strategists in the game.

Westhead lists a five year career coaching mark of 59-46, highlighted by his 1970-71 five capturing 20 of 27 contests, upsetting NCAA semifinalists Western Kentucky and Villanova, and participating in the NIT.

Last year, Westhead guided his young squad to a 18-10 record, which included triumphs over Princeton, Stanford, Western Kentucky, Niagara, Temple, Villanova & Rutgers.

Westhead began his career at Cheltenham high in 1964, gradually building a winning tradition, which culminated in the suburban Philadelphia school's first appearance ever in the P.I.A.A. state finals in 1968.

From 1968 to 1970, Westhead served as assistant athletic director at St. Joseph's College, and coached the 1969-70 Hawk freshmen to an unparalleled 21-2 season.

The Explorer coach added some additional credits during the summer of 1972 when he coached the Santurce team of the Puerto Rican 'Superior' league to a first place regular season finish. In the following summer, Westhead visited Bahia, Brazil to stage a court clinic as part of the state department's 'Partners of the Americas' exchange program.

A 1961 graduate of St. Joseph's College, Westhead received a master's degree from Villanova University in 1963, and had done some Ph.D. work at Temple University. He has also served on the English department faculties at Cheltenham high, St. Joseph's College, and La Salle College.

Westhead, his wife Cathy, and four children reside in Drexel Hill, Pa.

JOSEPH C. O'CONNOR
Assistant Coach

Joseph C. O'Connor, personable Explorer assistant coach, is primarily involved with scouting opponents and recruiting the stars of tomorrow.

As coach of the La Salle frosh from 1970 to 1972, Joe's squads compiled a 34-11 mark, highlighted by his '71-72 yearlings winning 20 of 23 contests.

The 32 year-old mentor with the knowledgeable basketball mind, is no stranger to this kind of success. As coach of South Jersey's Bishop Eustace Prep from 1966-70, O'Connor's amazing coaching log read 78-17, including the New Jersey State Championship in 1969.

O'Connor, a 1963 graduate of St. Joseph's College with a bachelor's degree in history, resides with his wife, Kathy, in Westbrook Park, Pa.

THE ATHLETE

The young man who accepts the exciting challenge of representing La Salle College on basketball courts throughout the nation will be one who recognizes that he is supplementing his classroom participation with athletic participation.

He will learn to discipline himself toward achieving a goal, to work in close association with other men, and to acquire judgment and responsibility. As such a student athlete, he will be, above all, a gentleman.

PAUL GALLAGHER
Assistant Coach

Paul Gallagher, a former Explorer varsity basketballer and later head coach at Drexel Hill, Pa.'s Monsignor Bonner High, returns for his fifth campaign as an assistant to coach Paul Westhead.

The 1964 graduate of La Salle served as an assistant coach at Bonner before becoming head coach at St. James High in Chester, Pa. in 1966-67. Gallagher returned to Bonner the following year, and went on to compile a brilliant 57-19 career coaching mark. His 1969-70 quintet finished with a fine 24-6 log, won Philadelphia's Catholic League Southern Division title and capped the season with the Alhambra Catholic Invitational trophy at Cumberland, Md.

Gallagher, 31, who captained Bonner's 1960 City Championship five, resides with his wife, Sue, and four children in Havertown, Pa.

DAVID A. (LEFTY) ERVIN
Assistant Coach

David "Lefty" Ervin is in his seventh season as an assistant basketball coach, and also distinguishes himself as an assistant baseball boss at La Salle.

While a student at the college, Lefty was a two-sport standout and co-captain of the Explorer baseball and basketball teams in his senior year. In 1968 he was honored with the Joseph Schmitz Jr. Award as the senior who best exemplified the high traditions of La Salle College in loyalty, sportsmanship and courage.

A starter on the basketball varsity as a sophomore, Ervin spent most of the next two years as the Explorers' sixth man and gained a reputation as one of the outstanding substitutes in the nation. He scored a total of 756 points for his career.

Lefty played baseball and basketball at Abington High before graduating in 1963.

Ervin, 28, his wife, Karen, and son, Joshua, reside in Cinnaminson, N.J.

THE LA SALLE COLLEGE ATHLETIC COMMITTEE

Dr. John J. Seydow, Associate Professor, English, Chairman
Dr. Thomas J. Lowery, Associate Professor, Biology
William J. Binkowski, Associate Professor, Education
Joseph L. Moran, Associate Professor, Spanish
Dr. Joseph C. Mihalich, Professor, Philosophy
Dr. Philip E. McGovern, Associate Professor, Political Science
Dr. Frank J. Schreiner, Associate Professor, Psychology
Joseph J. Sweeney, Alumni Representative
Thomas J. Conville, Jr., Alumni Representative
Marianne Gwiazdowski, Student Representative
Robert Guglielmi, Student Representative
Joseph B. Batory, Sports Information Director

EXPLORER 1974-75 PROSPECTS—

THE COACH'S VIEW

". . . our expectations are success orientated."
—Paul Westhead

With four starters returning including 6-5 senior All American candidate Bill Taylor and 6-10 junior Joe Bryant, we're quite optimistic about the 1974-75 season.

Taylor, the Big Five's scoring leader a year ago (19.7 ppg.), and Bryant, who made such a brilliant debut last season (18.7 ppg.-10.8 rpg.), give us the nucleus for an explosive attack.

In addition, our veteran junior guards, 6-0 Charlie Wise (11.9 ppg.) and 6-2 Glenn Collier (7.3 ppg.), offer experienced floor generalship.

One question mark to be solved is the replacement for graduated forward Joe DiCocco, whose all-around play in '73-74 gave us 10.5 ppg. and 9.4 rpg.

Veterans 6-8 junior Varick Cutler and 6-10 sophomore Donn Wilber are the leading candidates to fill that frontcourt vacancy.

We'll also be giving close scrutiny to frosh newcomers 6-6 Jim Wolkiewicz and 6-5 Gregg Metzinger.

In the backcourt, we lost some solid reserve personnel in Frank Moffatt and Steve Baruffi via graduation, but 6-0 soph Barry Brodzinski and 6-0 freshman Daryle Charles should give us the quality depth we require.

As in the past, we'll stress sound man-to-man defense and exert full court pressure quite frequently.

Our schedule is one of the most formidable ever at La Salle. We face tough road games at Notre Dame, Memphis State, Syracuse and Niagara, in addition to confronting major court powers Alabama, Furman and Houston in the Sugar Bowl Classic at New Orleans. The home card includes battles with Western Kentucky, Duquesne and Rutgers as well as Big Five foes.

Overall, we view 1974-75 as an exciting challenge, and our expectations are success orientated.

*Edward W. (Bill) Taylor
Senior 21 6-5 190 Forward
Tuskegee, Alabama

The Explorers' inconspicuous scoring machine is destined to become one of La Salle's top all-time point producers. A pre-season All American selection, Bill enters the 1974-75 campaign with 995 career points for an 18.7 ppg. two-year average. He's hit the double figure scoring column in 51 of 53 games, notching over 20 points on 20 different occasions.

Last season, the versatile sharpshooter tallied 551 points, leading all Big Five and MAC scorers with 19.7 ppg. Despite launching most of his shots from long range, Bill managed a fine 48.2% (242-502) from the floor. He highlighted the year with a career-high 39 point explosion vs. American U. canning 18 of 22 field goal attempts in one of the outstanding performances in the East in '74-75.

The poised forward had other superb endeavors as well, getting 28 points and 10 rebounds vs. St. Joseph's, 25 points and 12 rebounds (career-high) vs. Notre Dame, and 27 points and 9 rebounds vs. Wake Forest.

In his first varsity season as a soph, Bill registered 17.7 ppg. (444 points), only the fifth Explorer rookie in history to exceed 400 points.

He played his scholastic basketball at St. Francis Prep in Spring Grove, Pa. (coach Joe McGlynn) earning MVP honors in the Central Pennsylvania League as a senior.

Year	Games	Field Goals	Foul Goals	Rebounds	Points
1972-73	25	204	36	154	444
1973-74	28	242	67	197	551

°Joseph W. Bryant
Junior   20   6-10   200   Forward/Center
Philadelphia, Pa.

Joe unveiled a spectacular portfolio of offensive moves in his debut last year, racking up 486 points for an 18.7 ppg. average which was second only to teammate Bill Taylor in the MAC and Big Five. The only former La Salle player who produced more points in his rookie season was the legendary Tom Gola (504, 1951-52).

A mobile tower of talent, Joe also grabbed 282 rehounds in '73-74 to lead the Big Five and finish second in the MAC with 10.8 rpg.

'JB' was over 20 points in nine games with career highs of 37 points vs. Rider and 17 rebounds vs. Delaware, both in the conference playoffs. His other top efforts were 26 points and 13 rebounds vs. Niagara, 26 points and 10 rebounds vs. Canisius, and 22 points and 16 rebounds vs. Temple.

A high school All American, Joe was the most sought after big man in greater Philadelphia while at John Bartram high (coach Jack Farrell).

Year	Games	Field Goals	Foul Goals	Rebounds	Points
1973-74	26	200	86	282	486

°Barry D. Brodzinski
Sophomore 19 6-0 170 Guard
Philadelphia, Pa.

Barry appeared in only 11 varsity contests
uring 1973-74, scoring eight points and
rabbing eight rebounds for the season.
owever, the promising guard picked up
xperience on the Explorer sub-varsity,
veraging 18.6 ppg. and feeding a team-
igh 34 assists. His steady ball handling and
uperb long-range shooting capability could
ake him a key backcourt figure in this
ear's La Salle plans.

Barry was a former All City performer at
hiladelphia's North Catholic high (coach Tony Costantino) closing out
is career with 2053 points, the school's best ever.

ear	Games	Field Goals	Foul Goals	Rebounds	Points
973-74	11	3	2	8	8

Daryle L. Charles
Freshman 18 6-0 160 Guard
Jersey City, N.J.

Daryle averaged 17.0 ppg. and 9.0 rpg.
with an impressive seven assists per contest
as St. Anthony's (coach Bob Hurley) rolled
to a 30-0 slate and a second consecutive
New Jersey Parochial C title.

A persistent defender, Daryle compliments
his game with torrid outside marksmanship
and flashy passes. He was the MVP guard in
the 1974 Bridgeport, Connecticut All Star
contest in which New Jersey upset New York
City. His court credentials make him a very
positive backcourt addition to the '74-75
Explorers.

°Glenn N. Collier
Junior 20 6-2 150 Guard
Philadelphia, Pa.

Glenn became a starter in the Explorers'
eighth game of 1973-74, and the quick and
aggressive guard went on to record a fine
rookie campaign, contributing 7.3 ppg., 97
assists and a solid 52.2% (94-180) shooting
mark from the floor.

A creative passer who makes things hap-
pen, Glenn's top career game was vs. Lafayette when he scored 18 points, grabbed
seven rebounds, and passed off for 11 assists.

As a freshman, Glenn had led the sub-varsity point producers with 15.9
ppg. Previously, he enjoyed an outstanding scholastic basketball tenure
at West Catholic high, earning All Catholic honors (coach Bill Hoy).

Year	Games	Field Goals	Foul Goals.	Rebounds	Points
1973-74	28	94	16	60	204

John J. Connors
Junior 21 6-3 190 Forward
Drexel Hill, Pa.

A durable, physical swingman, John was a member of La Salle's best-ever '71-72 freshman squad (20-3), and in 1972-73 he started at a forward spot for the Sub-Varsity averaging 12.7 ppg.

John's credits also include two years as a frontline varsity golfer for the Explorers. A year ago, he worked full-time in business as part of La Salle's cooperative education program.

John was a standout scholastic court performer for coach Jim Purcell at Cardinal O'Hara high, and his dad, Mr. Jack Connors, is an assistant professor of sociology at the college.

*Varick F. Cutler
Junior 21 6-8 200 Forward
North Tonawanda, N.Y.

Varick hopefully will be fully recovered from a 1973 knee operation which limited his effectiveness last season. The powerful forward averaged 1.3 ppg. and 1.4 rpg. in nine varsity appearances getting a career-high four points and four rebounds vs. Biscayne. He also played on the Explorer sub-varsity leading the team in scoring (22.3 ppg.) and rebounding (9.7 rpg.).

A tough outside shooter, Varick transferred to La Salle from the University of Maryland after averaging 15.2 ppg. and 8.4 rpg. for an outstanding 1971-72 Terp frosh squad.

The former high school All American had a brilliant career at North Tonawanda high (coach Ted More).

Year	Games	Field Goals	Foul Goals	Rebounds	Points
1973-74	9	5	2	13	12

A Backcourt Quartet (From Left): Collier, Wise, Brodzinski and Char

Gregg D. Metzinger
Freshman **18 6-5 200** Forward
Barrington, N.J.

This All South Jersey frontcourter rolled up exceptional stats of 22.0 ppg. and 12.0 rpg. at Paul VI high in Haddon Township, N.J. (coach Art DiPatri) during '73-74.

A deadly streak shooter, Gregg is a confident hustler who is deceptively strong. In last year's New Jersey Parochial State Tourney, he bombed in 44 points vs. the Christian Brothers' Academy.

His great hunger and desire for the game should guarantee his development into a first class collegiate swingman.

Joseph A. Mihalich
Freshman **18 6-0 165** Guard
Philadelphia, Pa.

A typical 'Philadelphia' guard, Joe is a fundamentally sound backcourt ace, who complements his overall game with relentless defense. With varsity exposure, Joe could develop into a real plus for the Explorers. He played his high school B-Ball at La Salle under coach Mike Osborne, and earned All-Catholic honors in 1974. His father, Dr. Joseph Mihalich, is a Philosophy professor at the college.

°Donn K. Wilber
Sophomore **19 6-10 200** Center
Radnor, Pa.

Donn averaged 2.6 ppg. and 1.1 rpg. in seven varsity games as a frontcourt reserve, registering a career-best nine points and five rebounds vs. Villanova. A defensive intimidator, he also managed 11.7 ppg. and 7.8 rpg. for the La Salle sub-varsity. Donn has the size and agility to become a frontcourt fixture for the Explorers in years to come.

A better than average scholastic high jumper, he played his high school basketball at Upper Merion (coach Al Cornish).

Year	Games	Field Goals	Foul Goals	Rebounds!	Points
1973-74	7	6	6	8	18

13

°Charles E. Wise
Junior 20 6-0 155 Guard
Cape May, N.J.

The perfect combination of playmaker and scorer, 'Sweet Charlie' led the '73-74 Explorers in assists (110) and averaged 11.9 ppg. on 51.2% accuracy from the field.

Charlie hit a career-high 19 points vs. Pennsylvania, Western Kentucky, Stanford and Delaware last year. He also set personal bests of eight assists vs. Holy Cross and Lafayette, and six rebounds vs. Manhattan.

The Big Five's premier defensive wizard, Charlie's numerous steals over the past two seasons have created many La Salle baskets.

A former football standout at Lower Cape May Regional high, Charlie also was an All South Jersey basketball sensation (coach George Holden).

Year	Games	Field Goals	Foul Goals	Rebounds	Points
1972-73	14	40	19	36	99
1973-74	28	148	39	80	335

James D. Wolkiewicz
Freshman 18 6-6 185 Forward
Philadelphia, Pa.

Jim seldom got headline coverage at North Catholic high (coach Tony Costantino) but the tenacious frontcourter has been a complete player doing many things well on the court.

Consistent off the boards, Jim battled underneath for 16.0 ppg. and 18.0 rpg. as a senior in '73-74.

With the ability to make the big play under pressure and perform well in the clutch, Jim seems destined for success.

OPPONENT X-RAYS

1. THE UNITED STATES MILITARY ACADEMY

Friday, November 29, 1974, 9:15 P.M., at the Palestra,
Philadelphia, Pa.

SERIES RECORD:
La Salle 2, Army 0

Coach Dan Dougherty
(Three Years, 28-44)

OUTLOOK: The Cadets have two steady veteran forwards in 6-5 senior Dave Thomas (7.7 ppg.-5.0 rpg.) and 6-5 soph Rich Crump (9.1 ppg.) and hope for improvement from 6-8 soph pivotman Eric Schlossberg (5.3 ppg.). At the guard positions, 5-10 junior Bill Walsh (5.5 ppg.) will be joined by 6-0 soph Bobby Jones (22.0 ppg.-JV), who transferred from La Salle a year ago. Disciplined offense, aggressive defense will create problems for opponents.

Location: West Point, N.Y. 10996
Enrollment: 4200
Conference: Independent
Publicity: Bob Kinney
Office Phone: 914-938-3303

Nickname: Cadets
Colors: Black, Gold & Gray
1973-74 Record: 6-18
Lettermen: Returning 4, Lost 4
Captain: Dave Thomas

Year by Year Scores
1972-73 La Salle 73-63
1973-74 La Salle 83-71

2. LEHIGH UNIVERSITY

Wednesday, December 4, 1974, 8:00 P.M., at Grace Hall,
Bethlehem, Pa.

SERIES RECORD:
La Salle 8, Lehigh 1

Coach Tom Pugliese
(Two Years, 11-38)

OUTLOOK: The Engineers played five freshmen regularly last year and should be ready to collect some dividends. 6-0 soph Steve Zambo (14.1 ppg.), and 6-0 soph Rich Price (8.1 ppg.) can score from outside, and 6-7 soph Charlie Brown (12.7 ppg.-7.8 rpg.) is a quality forward. Sophs 6-2 Dick Packer (6.2 ppg.) and 6-7 Doug Kistler (4.8 ppg.-4.0 rpg.) are other key returnees. Loaded with young players; could still be a year away.

Location: Bethlehem, Pa. 18015
Enrollment: 3800
Conference: East Coast (West)
Publicity: Joe Whritenour
Office Phone: 215-691-7000 Ext. 793

Nickname: Engineers
Colors: Brown & White
1973-74 Record: 3-21
Lettermen: Returning 8, Lost 1
Captain(s): TBA

Year by Year Scores
1958-59 La Salle 81-47	1963-64 La Salle 68-40
1959-60 La Salle 86-54	1971-72 Lehigh 69-64
1960-61 La Salle 77-62	1972-73 La Salle 75-59
1961-62 La Salle 71-59	1973-74 La Salle 87-37
1962-63 La Salle 85-34	

3. BISCAYNE COLLEGE

Saturday, December 7, 1974, 9:15 P.M., at the Palestra, Philadelphia, Pa.

SERIES RECORD:
La Salle 2, Biscayne 1

OUTLOOK: The offense-minded Bobcats have two explosive sophomores, 6-4 Art Collins (20.8 ppg.-9.6 rpg.) and 6-4 Ed Zukowski (19.4 ppg.-8.1 rpg.) and will welcome 6-9 frosh Kevin Fussell, their tallest player ever. 6-0 soph Sam Williams (8.2 ppg.) and 6-4 senior Larry Mokar (7.5 ppg.) provide a good backcourt nucleus. 6-3 transfer Bob Valibus and 6-6 frosh Maurice Thurston could surprise. Enough experience and talent here to be respected!

Coach Ken Stibler
(Eight Years, 100-91)

Location: Miami, Fla. 33054
Enrollment: 350
Conference: Independent
Publicity: Roy H. Slanhoff
Office Phone: 305-625-1561 Ext. 140

Nickname: Bobcats
Colors: Columbia Blue, Navy & White
1973-74 Record: 10-13
Lettermen: Returning 7, Lost 4
Captain(s): Arthur Collins & Ed Zukowski

Year by Year Scores

1971-72	Biscayne	103-93
1972-73	La Salle	69-67
1973-74	La Salle	97-75

4. LAFAYETTE COLLEGE

Wednesday, December 11, 1974, 8:00 P.M., at the Alumni Memorial Gym, Easton, Pa.

SERIES RECORD:
La Salle 23, Lafayette 6

OUTLOOK: The Leopard wealth is counted in guards with 6-2 senior Frank DiLeo (13.7 ppg.), 6-2 junior Todd Tripucka (9.3 ppg.) and 6-0 junior Gerry Kavanaugh (4.5 ppg.) leading this year's attack. 6-6 senior Henry Horne (7.2 ppg.-7.6 rpg.) is sound at one forward spot with sophs 6-7 Kris Grundberg (15.8 ppg.-22.4 rpg.-frosh) and 6-5 Tom Goodman (12.9 ppg.-13.1 rpg.-frosh) being tabbed to fill the frontcourt void. This team figures to gain strength as the season progresses.

Coach Tom Davis
(Three Years, 54-25)

Location: Easton, Pa. 18042
Enrollment: 1900
Conference: East Coast (West)
Publicity: Rich Mazzuto
Office Phone: 215-253-8802

Nickname: Leopards
Colors: Maroon & White
1973-74 Record: 17-9
Lettermen: Returning 6, Lost 4
Captain(s): Henry Horne & Frank DiLeo

Year by Year Scores

1944-45	Lafayette	52-45	1961-62	Lafayette	73-64
1945-46	Lafayette	57-49	1962-63	La Salle	95-59
1947-48	La Salle	43-39	1963-64	La Salle	100-86
1948-49	La Salle	61-37	1964-65	La Salle	91-73
1950-51	La Salle	71-64	1965-66	Lafayette	93-81
1951-52	La Salle	62-52 (OT)	1966-67	La Salle	85-72
1952-53	La Salle	56-50	1967-68	La Salle	74-75
1953-54	La Salle	88-70	1968-69	La Salle	97-65
1954-55	La Salle	76-60	1969-70	La Salle	102-73
1955-56	La Salle	95-81	1970-71	La Salle	93-82
1956-57	Lafayette	84-75	1970-71	La Salle	74-71
1957-58	La Salle	82-74	1971-72	Lafayette	86-66
1958-59	La Salle	84-77	1972-73	Lafayette	77-68
1959-60	La Salle	81-73	1973-74	La Salle	87-66
1960-61	La Salle	104-86			

5. HOLY CROSS COLLEGE

Saturday, December 14, 1974, 7:15 P.M., at the Palestra, Philadelphia, Pa.

OUTLOOK: A veteran returning frontcourt of 6-9 junior Marty Halsey (12.5 ppg.-7.1 rpg.), 6-7 junior Jim Dee (12.5 ppg.-6.5 rpg.), and 6-5 soph Jim Gooch (8.6 ppg.) will be bolstered by talented frosh newcomers 6-6 Chris Potter and 6-5 Michael Vicens. 6-2 senior Joe Carballeira (8.8 ppg.) will likely be joined by 5-11 frosh Jose Martinez in the backcourt. The Cross should be greatly improved over a year ago.

Coach George Blaney
(Two Years, 17-35)

Location: Worcester, Mass. 01610
Enrollment: 2400
Conference: Independent
Publicity: Rich Lewis
Office Phone: 617-793-2571 or 2583

Nickname: Crusaders
Colors: Royal Purple
1973-74 Record: 8-18
Lettermen: Returning 10, Lost 3
Captain(s): Doug Downey & Dave Holland

Year by Year Scores

1948-49 La Salle 63-61	1973-74 La Salle 94-80
1971-72 Holy Cross.... 85-79	

6. CANISIUS COLLEGE

Wednesday, December 18, 1974, 9:15 P.M., at the Palestra, Philadelphia, Pa.

OUTLOOK: All five 1973-74 starters will be back led by the nation's top scorer of a year ago 6-5 junior Larry Fogle (33.4 ppg.-14.0 rpg.). 6-6 junior Ken Lee (14.7 ppg.), 6-8 junior Charley Jordan (15.3 ppg.-10.2 rpg.), 5-11 senior Mike Roberts (12.2 ppg.) and 6-0 senior Jim Schofield (6.8 ppg., 198 assists) guarantee an explosive offense. The Griffins will be golden!

Coach John McCarthy
(First Year)

Location: Buffalo, N.Y. 14208
Enrollment: 3000
Conference: ECAC
Publicity: Mike Barth
Office Phone: 716-883-7000 Ext. 338

Nickname: Golden Griffins
Colors: Blue & Gold
1973-74 Record: 14-12
Lettermen: Returning 10, Lost 0
Captain(s): TBA

Year by Year Scores

1940-41 La Salle 42-37	1965-66 La Salle 95-81
1948-49 La Salle 59-43	1966-67 Canisius 93-75
1954-55 La Salle 99-64	1967-68 La Salle 80-64
1958-59 La Salle 77-64	1968-69 La Salle 68-56
1959-60 La Salle 82-68	1969-70 Canisius 80-70
1960-61 Canisius 94-73	1970-71 La Salle 92-55
1961-62 La Salle 73-63	1971-72 La Salle 80-78
1962-63 Canisius 76-53	1972-73 La Salle 96-85
1963-64 La Salle 91-81	1973-74 Canisius 89-81

THE DAYTON INVITATIONAL
BASKETBALL TOURNAMENT

(Games 7 & 8)
Friday, December 20, and Saturday, December 21, 1974
at the University of Dayton Arena, Dayton, Ohio.

FIRST ROUND, Friday, December 20, 1974

LA SALLE vs. Clemson ....7:00 P.M.
Texas Tech vs. Dayton ....9:00 P.M.

FINAL ROUND, Saturday, December 21, 1974

Consolation Game (Matching the First Round Losers) ....7:00 P.M.
Championship Game (Matching the First Round Winners) ......9:00 P.M.

7. CLEMSON UNIVERSITY

Friday, December 20, 1974, 7:00 P.M. at the
University of Dayton Arena, Dayton, Ohio
OPENING ROUND OF THE DAYTON INVITATIONAL

SERIES RECORD:
First Meeting

OUTLOOK: The Tigers feature a rapidly-improving potential superstar in 7-1 soph Wayne 'Tree' Rollins, who notched 12.4 ppg. and 12.2 rpg. in his debut last year. Seniors 6-2 Van Gregg (13.8 ppg.) and 6-9 240 lb. Wayne Croft (11.2 ppg.-8.0 rpg.) provide a nucleus of experience. Four 'blue chip' frosh, 6-6 Colon Abraham, 6-6 Jim Howell, 6-5 Stan Rome and 6-4 Skip Wise, should also make significant contributions. The Clemson cage program is on the move!

Coach Tates Locke
(Four Years, 45-59)

Location: Clemson, S.C. 29631
Enrollment: 10,400
Conference: Atlantic Coast
Publicity: Bob Bradley
Office Phone: 803-654-4111 or 656-2101

Nickname: Tigers
Colors: Purple & Orange
1973-74 Record: 14-12
Lettermen: Returning 9, Lost 2
Captain(s): Game Captains

THE UNIVERSITY OF DAYTON
(Possible Dayton Invitational Opponent)

SERIES RECORD:
La Salle 3, Dayton 1

OUTLOOK: Six lettermen return from a club which destroyed Notre Dame during the 1973-74 regular season, and extended UCLA to triple overtime before bowing in the NCAA western regionals. 6-2 soph Johnny Davis (14.3 ppg.), and seniors 6-8 Allen Elijah (10.7 ppg.-10.0 rpg.), 6-8 Joe Fisher and 6-5 Jim Testerman are capable vets. Incoming frosh 6-4 Joe Siggins, 6-2 Greg Holloway and 6-9 Ervin Giddings will help the cause. Pointing toward a balanced attack which will give most opponents trouble.

Coach Don Donoher
(Ten Years, 194-87)

Location: Dayton, Ohio 45469
Enrollment: 5900
Conference: Independent
Publicity: Joe Mitch
Office Phone: 513-229-4421

Nickname: Flyers
Colors: Red & Blue
1973-74 Record: 20-9
Lettermen: Returning 6, Lost 3
Captain(s): TBA

Year by Year Scores

1951-52 La Salle	75-64	1953-54 La Salle	82-58
1952-53 La Salle	73-64	1961-62 Dayton	81-67

TEXAS TECH
(Possible Dayton Invitational Opponent)

SERIES RECORD:
First Meeting

OUTLOOK: The Red Raider frontcourt is intact with 6-9 junior center Rick Bullock (21.4 ppg.-10.7 rpg.) flanked by 6-6 juniors Willie Johnson (16.2 ppg.-8.9 rpg.) and Grady Newton (8.1 ppg.). Junior college transfers 6-9 Stanley Lee and 6-6 Rudy Liggins are welcome additions. 6-3 senior Phil Bailey (7.5 ppg.) is the only guard with heavy varsity exposure. Last year's Southwest Conference runner-up could be this season's favorite!

Coach Gerald Myers
(Four Years, 58-34)

Location: Lubbock, TX 79409
Enrollment: 21,500
Conference: Southwest
Publicity: Ralph Carpenter
Office Phone: 806-742-4141

Nickname: Red Raiders
Colors: Scarlet & Black
1973-74 Record: 17-9
Lettermen: Returning 7, Lost 2
Captain(s): TBA

THE SUGAR BOWL BASKETBALL CLASSIC
(Games 9 & 10)
Sunday, December 29, and Monday, December 30, 1974
at the Municipal Auditorium, New Orleans, La.

FIRST ROUND, Sunday, December 29, 1974

Furman vs. LA SALLE ....7:00 P.M.
Alabama vs. Houston ....9:00 P.M.

FINAL ROUND, Monday, December 30, 1974

Consolation Game (Matching First Round Losers) ....7:00 P.M.
Championship Game (Matching First Round Winners) ....9:00 P.M.

9. FURMAN UNIVERSITY
Sunday, December 29, 1974, 7:00 P.M. at the
Municipal Auditorium, New Orleans, La.
OPENING ROUND OF SUGAR BOWL CLASSIC

SERIES RECORD:
La Salle 2, Furman 0

OUTLOOK: The Paladins have back all the key personnel from last year's 22-9 club which stunned South Carolina in the NCAA eastern regionals, including 6-9 All American candidate Clyde 'Marvelous' Mayes (17.3 ppg.-13.0 rpg.), 7-1 pivotman Fessor 'Moose' Leonard (15.3 ppg.-7.7 rpg.) and steady 6-6 Craig Lynch (9.8 ppg.-5.4 rpg.) round out an impressive frontcourt. At one guard spot, Furman offers 6-1 Bruce Grimm (14.4 ppg.) who's been compared to Gail Goodrich, with 5-10 veteran playmaker Baron Hill having the inside track on the other backcourt position. This team has the horses to be in the thick of the national picture.

Coach Joe Williams
(Four Years, 74-41)

Location: Greenville, S.C. 29613
Enrollment: 2,089
Conference: Southern
Publicity: Charlie Dayton
Office Phone: 803-246-3550 Ext. 359

Nickname: Paladins
Colors: Purple & White
1973-74 Record: 22-9
Lettermen: Returning 6, Lost 4
Captain(s): TBA

Year by Year Scores
1953-54 La Salle 100-83
1955-56 La Salle 73-65

THE UNIVERSITY OF HOUSTON
(Possible Sugar Bowl Opponent)

SERIES RECORD:
First Meeting

OUTLOOK: The Cougars only won 17 of 26 a year ago, but shed no tears. 6-9 All American Louis Dunbar (21.7 ppg.-8.5 rpg.) will be flanked by fellow frontcourt returnees 6-10 Maurice Presley (14.2 ppg.-10.4 rpg.) and 6-9 David Marrs (9.3 ppg.-6.7 rpg.). Coach Guy Lewis has one tough guard back in 6-3 Otis Birdsong (14.3 ppg.) and will find another from a long list of blue chip recruits. A tradition as one of the court powers of the Southwest will be upheld by the Houston five this season.

Coach Guy Lewis
(18 Years, 338-157)

Location: Houston, Tx. 77004
Enrollment: 27,000
Conference: Southwest
    (Eligible for title competition
    in 1975-76)
Publicity: Ted Nance
Office Phone: 713-748-6844

Nickname: Cougars
Colors: Scarlet & White
1973-74 Record: 17-9
Lettermen: Returning 7, Lost 4
Captain(s): TBA

UNIVERSITY OF ALABAMA
(Possible Sugar Bowl Opponent)

SERIES RECORD:
First Meeting

OUTLOOK: 6-5 Charles Cleveland (17.1 ppg.-8.4 rpg.) and 6-10 Leon Douglas (15.2 ppg.-9.9 rpg.) did it all a year ago as C. M. Newton's five posted a 22-4 record and second place finish in the Southeastern Conference. The Crimson Tide rolled over Kentucky and Tennessee twice, lost two games to league titlist Vanderbilt by a total of three points. 6-6 Charles Russell (11.0 ppg.-5.8 rpg.), 6-4 T. R. Dunn (9.4 ppg.-8.0 rpg.), and 6-9 Rickey Brown (7.3 ppg.) add loads of depth. Top ten material here!

Coach C. M. Newton
(Six Years, 84-74)

Location: Tuscaloosa, Ala. 35401
Enrollment: 13,835
Conference: Southeastern
Publicity: Charley Thornton
Office Phone: 205-348-6084

Nickname: Crimson Tide
Colors: Crimson & White
1973-74 Record: 22-4
Lettermen: Returning 6, Lost 1
Captain: Charles Cleveland

11. HOFSTRA UNIVERSITY

Saturday, January 4, 1975, 8:00 P.M., at the Palestra, Philadelphia, Pa.

SERIES RECORD:
La Salle 5, Hofstra 1

Coach Roger Gaeckler
(Two Years, 16-32)

OUTLOOK: Soph forwards 6-5 Rich Laurel (18.8 ppg.-6.9 rpg.) and 6-6 Pat Kammerer (9.4 ppg.-6.2 rpg.) and 6-8 senior Vince Volmut (7.3 ppg.) are capable frontcourt veterans, and transfers 6-9 John Irving and 6-6 Bob Bush should have an impact. 6-6 Bernard Tomlin and 6-1 Arnold Coleman, another pair of transfers, will challenge 6-2 soph Ken Rood (12.2 ppg.) in the backcourt. An optimistic picture sees the Dutchmen becoming a legitimate power.

Location: Hempstead, L.I., N.Y. 11550
Enrollment: 6200
Conference: East Coast (East)
Publicity: Erich Linker
Office Phone: 516-560-3578 or 3466

Nickname: Flying Dutchmen
Colors: Blue & Gold
1973-74 Record: 8-16
Lettermen: Returning 10, Lost 1
Captain(s): TBA

Year by Year Scores

1968-69 La Salle 89-68	1971-72 Hofstra 58-56
1969-70 La Salle 83-64	1972-73 La Salle 76-55
1970-71 La Salle 79-62	1973-74 La Salle 66-53

THE PALESTRA

12. MEMPHIS STATE UNIVERSITY

Wednesday, January 8, 1975, 8:00 P.M., at the Mid-South Coliseum, Memphis, Tenn.

SERIES RECORD:
First Meeting

OUTLOOK: 6-4 soph Dexter Reed (18.4 ppg.) led the Tigers in scoring in '73-74, and he'll be rejoined by fellow starters 6-5 Bill Cook (16.2 ppg.) and 6-6 Clarence Jones (10.2 ppg.), both juniors. Other key veterans are juniors 6-10 John Washington (6.2 ppg.-7.8 rpg.) and 6-7 Ed Wilson (4.1 ppg.). 6-9 frosh John Gunn and 6-9 junior college transfer Marion Hillard are expected to be heard from. A great winning tradition is hardly in trouble this year!

Coach Wayne Yates
(First Year)

Location: Memphis, Tenn. 38152
Enrollment: 22,000
Conference: Independent
Publicity: Jack Bugbee
Office Phone: 901-454-2337

Nickname: Tigers
Colors: Blue & Gray
1973-74 Record: 19-11
Lettermen: Returning 8, Lost 4
Captain(s): TBA

13. NIAGARA UNIVERSITY

Saturday, January 11, 1975, 8:00 P.M., at the Niagara Falls Convention Center, Niagara University, N.Y.

SERIES RECORD:
La Salle 15, Niagara 13

OUTLOOK: The Purple Eagle frontcourt is solid with juniors 6-4 Andy Walker (17.5 ppg.-7.9 rpg.), 6-10 Mike Hanley (9.2 ppg.-7.3 rpg.), and 6-8 Bruce Watson (8.0 ppg.-5.6 rpg.) back once again. Promising frosh 6-8 Vern Allen adds even more power to the frontline. Philadelphian Chico Singleton (8.5 ppg.) is a 6-1 soph who will 'do it all' at one guard spot while the other backcourt position is up for grabs. A deep veteran team on the rise!

Coach Frank Layden
(Six Years, 89-71)

Location: Niagara Univ., N.Y. 14109
Enrollment: 3,585
Conference: Independent
Publicity: TBA
Office Phone: 716-285-1212 Ext. 344

Nickname: Purple Eagles
Colors: Purple & White
1973-74 Record: 12-14
Lettermen: Returning 10, Lost 1
Captain(s): TBA

Year by Year Scores

1933-34	Niagara	33-28	1961-62 Niagara	78-64
1941-42	Niagara	40-37	1962-63 Niagara	79-76
1950-51	La Salle	82-56	1963-64 La Salle	58-54
1951-52	La Salle	85-74	1964-65 La Salle	67-59 (OT)
1952-53	La Salle	87-76	1965-66 Niagara	88-87 (OT)
1953-54	Niagara	69-50	1966-67 Niagara	72-69
1953-54	Niagara	74-66	1966-67 La Salle	86-72
1954-55	La Salle	76-75	1967-68 Niagara	100-83
1955-56	Niagara	72-70	1968-69 La Salle	88-73
1956-57	La Salle	83-74	1969-70 La Salle	101-90
1957-58	La Salle	69-68 (OT)	1970-71 La Salle	96-79
1958-59	Niagara	72-56	1971-72 Niagara	71-70
1959-60	La Salle	64-48	1972-73 La Salle	80-72
1960-61	Niagara	77-71	1973-74 La Salle	67-65

14. ST. JOSEPH'S COLLEGE

Wednesday, January 15, 1975, 9:15 P.M., at the Palestra, Philadelphia, Pa.

SERIES RECORD:
La Salle 35, St. Joseph's 37

OUTLOOK: 6-7 senior Ron Righter (12.1 ppg.-6.3 rpg.) is the only returning starter, but 6-0 senior Fran Rafferty (2.5 ppg.) has seen plenty of action as a key reserve in the past. Some quality recruits include freshmen 6-5 Mike Thomas, 6-3 John Willcox and 6-0 Mike Hurley, each of whom could help immediately. 6-10 junior John Snyder, and sophs 6-7 Steve Vassalotti and 6-6 Lee Scott are the other leading candidates. Should be the typical hustling, aggressive St. Joe team.

Coach Harry Booth
(First Year)

Location: Philadelphia, Pa. 19131
Enrollment: 2,175
Conference: East Coast (East)
Publicity: Andy Dougherty
Office Phone: 215-879-1000

Nickname: Hawks
Colors: Crimson & Gray
1973-74 Record: 19-11
Lettermen: Returning 5, Lost 7
Captain(s): TBA

Year by Year Scores

1900-01	La Salle 32- 7	1948-49	La Salle 78-41
1900-01	La Salle 29-13	1949-50	La Salle 79-59
1901-02	La Salle 70- 8	1949-50	La Salle 74-53
1910	La Salle 22-18	1950-51	La Salle 77-64
1910	St. Joseph's .. 24-18	1950-51	La Salle 81-63
1910	St. Joseph's .. 35-29	1951-52	St. Joseph's .. 54-53
1911	La Salle 10- 6	1951-52	La Salle 68-50
1911	La Salle 20-16	1952-53	La Salle 79-52
1912	La Salle .... N/A	1952-53	La Salle 75-63
1915-16	St. Joseph's .. 31-26	1953-54	La Salle 73-57
1915-16	La Salle 29-21	1953-54	La Salle 78-64
1916-17	La Salle 30-29	1954-55	La Salle 82-56
1916-17	St. Joseph's .. 28-27	1955-56	St. Joseph's .. 69-56
1916-17	La Salle 22-17	1956-57	St. Joseph's .. 97-85 (OT)
1922-23	St. Joseph's .. 44- 9	1956-57	La Salle 61-57
1933-34	La Salle 27-15	1957-58	St. Joseph's .. 82-77 (OT)
1933-34	La Salle 39-20	1958-59	St. Joseph's .. 70-63
1934-35	St. Joseph's .. 28-25	1959-60	La Salle 80-73
1934-35	La Salle 32-25	1960-61	St. Joseph's .. 65-54
1934-35	St. Joseph's .. 26-25	1961-62	La Salle 72-71
1935-36	St. Joseph's .. 23-19	1962-63	St. Joseph's .. 66-49
1935-36	St. Joseph's .. 40-20	1963-64	La Salle 80-70
1936-37	St. Joseph's .. 25-21	1964-65	St. Joseph's .. 93-85
1936-37	St. Joseph's .. 28-25	1965-66	St. Joseph's .. 92-69
1937-38	La Salle 22-18	1966-67	St. Joseph's .. 96-85
1938-39	La Salle 32-31	1966-67	La Salle 73-70
1939-40	St. Joseph's .. 33-28	1967-68	La Salle 103-71
1940-41	St. Joseph's .. 48-40	1968-69	La Salle 84-67
1941-42	St. Joseph's .. 58-53	1969-70	St. Joseph's 101-99 (2 OT)
1942-43	St. Joseph's .. 48-45	1970-71	St. Joseph's .. 66-56
1943-44	St. Joseph's .. 53-33	1970-71	St. Joseph's .. 81-76 (OT)
1943-44	St. Joseph's .. 53-37	1971-72	St. Joseph's .. 72-55
1944-45	St. Joseph's .. 39-36	1972-73	St. Joseph's 77-52
1945-46	La Salle 38-36	1972-73	St. Joseph's 68-55
1946-47	La Salle 48-45	1973-74	St. Joseph's 75-73
1947-48	St. Joseph's .. 70-65	1973-74	St. Joseph's 76-71

15. UNIVERSITY OF PENNSYLVANIA

Saturday, January 18, 1975, 8:45 P.M., at the Palestra, Philadelphia, Pa.

SERIES RECORD:
La Salle 11, Pennsylvania 16

OUTLOOK: The Quakers return the key members of the cast responsible for a fifth straight NCAA appearance last year. 6-8 senior All American candidate Ron Haigler (17.4 ppg.-10.6 rpg.), 6-8 junior John Engles (14.1 ppg.-8.3 rpg.) and 6-11 junior Henry Johnson (5.6 ppg.-5.3 rpg.) are more than formidable upfront. In addition, 6-1 junior All Ivy guard John Beecroft (9.8 ppg.) will be joined by 6-4 super-soph Mark Lonetto (22.0 ppg.-fresh) in the backcourt. A national powerhouse!

Coach **Chuck Daly**
(Three Years, 67-16)

Location: Philadelphia, Pa. 19104
Enrollment: 6,935
Conference: Ivy League
Publicity: Edwin S. Fabricius
Office Phone: 215-594-6128

Nickname: Quakers
Colors: Red & Blue
1973-74 Record: 21-6
Lettermen: Returning 11, Lost 3
Captain: Ron Haigler

Year by Year Scores

1933-34 Penn	35-22	1961-62 La Salle 69-57
1934-35 Penn	33-22	1962-63 Penn 78-74
1935-36 Penn	36-28	1963-64 La Salle 61-58
1936-37 Penn	36-28	1964-65 La Salle 78-64
1946-47 Penn	68-56	1965-66 Penn 90-76
1947-48 La Salle	55-43	1966-67 La Salle 85-83
1948-49 La Salle	64-44	1967-68 Penn 57-45
1951-52 La Salle	75-58	1968-69 La Salle 78-64
1955-56 La Salle	64-52	1969-70 Penn 76-67
1956-57 La Salle	84-73	1970-71 Penn 107-88
1957-58 Penn	67-66 (OT)	1971-72 Penn 80-66
1958-59 Penn	73-70	1972-73 Penn 57-45
1959-60 Penn	66-62	1972-73 Penn 57-45
1960-61 La Salle	67-63	1973-74 Penn 84-82

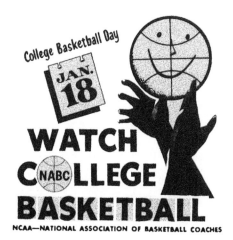

College Basketball Day

JAN. 18

WATCH C(NABC)LLEGE BASKETBALL

NCAA—NATIONAL ASSOCIATION OF BASKETBALL COACHES

16. WEST CHESTER STATE COLLEGE

Tuesday, January 21, 1975, 7:15 P.M., at the Palestra, Philadelphia, Pa.

SERIES RECORD:
La Salle 28, West Chester 6

OUTLOOK: The Rams have 6-4 senior Jerry DuVall (13.7 ppg.-12.1 rpg.) and 6-6 soph Curt Conrad (10.7 ppg.-6.2 rpg.) back on the frontline, and will add 6-5 transfer Bill Kauffman. 5-11 sophomore Paul McShane (7.7 ppg.) and 6-2 senior Ed Levandowski (7.9 ppg.) should get the job done in the guard spots. Lacking good size, this club hopes to compensate with aggressiveness and quickness.

Coach Earl Voss
(One Year, 11-15)

Location: West Chester, Pa. 19380
Enrollment: 6,438
Conference: East Coast (East)
Publicity: Bob Nye
Office Phone: 215-436-2749

Nickname: Golden Rams
Colors: Purple & Gold
1973-74 Record: 11-15
Lettermen: Returning 7, Lost 1
Captain: Jerry DuVall

Year by Year Scores

1931-32 La Salle	38-20	1951-52 La Salle	85-55
1931-32 West Chester	18-15	1952-53 La Salle	111-60
1932-33 La Salle	30-27	1953-54 La Salle	65-51
1932-33 La Salle	32-30	1954-55 La Salle	85-50
1933-34 La Salle	37-23	1955-56 La Salle	90-78
1933-34 La Salle	25-24	1956-57 La Salle	57-51
1935-36 West Chester	39-20	1957-58 La Salle	68-66
1935-36 West Chester	36-30	1958-59 La Salle	85-67
1936-37 La Salle	39-24	1959-60 La Salle	85-68
1936-37 West Chester	28-27	1960-61 La Salle	83-67
1937-38 La Salle	47-34	1967-68 La Salle	79-55
1937-38 West Chester	33-30	1968-69 La Salle	91-73
1938-39 La Salle	46-31	1969-70 La Salle	92-80
1938-39 La Salle	48-45	1970-71 La Salle	82-68
1939-40 La Salle	37-21	1971-72 La Salle	86-62
1939-40 West Chester	30-27	1972-73 La Salle	92-52
1940-41 La Salle	43-31	1973-74 La Salle	73-53

17. DUQUESNE UNIVERSITY

Friday, January 24, 1975, 9:15 P.M., at the Palestra, Philadelphia, Pa.

SERIES RECORD:
La Salle 11, Duquesne 14

OUTLOOK: The Dukes' fortunes rest in the veteran hands of seniors 6-6 Kip McLane (13.1 ppg.-9.1 rpg.) and 6-2 Oscar Jackson (8.4 ppg.) along with 6-5 junior Roland Jones (11.0 ppg.-5.8 rpg.) and 6-2 soph Norm Nixon (10.7 ppg.). Jack Yun and Bernie O'Keefe are capable 6-4 seniors and 6-9 junior Ray Milligan could be ready to blossom. 6-8 sophs John Werner and Don Cambridge may help upfront. A physically-tough competitive quintet!

Coach John Cinicola
(First Year)

Location: Pittsburgh, Pa. 15219
Enrollment: 8,000
Conference: Independent
Publicity: Clair N. Brown
Office Phone: 412-434-6565

Nickname: Dukes
Colors: Red & Blue
1973-74 Record: 12-12
Lettermen: Returning 8, Lost 4
Captain(s): Don McLane & Oscar Jackson

Year by Year Scores

1939-40 Duquesne ...... 27-23 (OT)	1962-63 La Salle 73-69
1949-50 Duquesne 49-47	1963-64 Duquesne 89-58
1950-51 Duquesne 53-43	1964-65 La Salle 83-69
1951-52 Duquesne 71-60	1965-66 Duquesne 79-77
1951-52 La Salle 59-46	1966-67 La Salle 77-66
1952-53 La Salle 74-66	1967-68 La Salle .... 80-79 (OT)
1954-55 Duquesne 67-65	1968-69 La Salle 85-71
1956-57 La Salle 87-80	1969-70 Duquesne 67-64
1957-58 Duquesne 74-55	1970-71 Duquesne 95-86
1958-59 La Salle 72-65	1971-72 Duquesne 81-69
1959-60 La Salle 68-65	1972-73 La Salle 69-67
1960-61 Duquesne 78-63	1973-74 Duquesne 81-63
1961-62 Duquesne 80-66	

18. WESTERN KENTUCKY UNIVERSITY

Wednesday, January 29, 1975, 7:15 P.M., at the Palestra, Philadelphia, Pa.

Coach Jim Richards
(Three Years, 40-37)

SERIES RECORD:
La Salle 9, Western Kentucky 14

OUTLOOK: The Hilltoppers' guard strength, 6-2 junior Johnny Britt (18.4 ppg.), 6-1 junior Chuck Rawlings (13.2 ppg.) and 5-10 senior Calvin Wade (10.4 ppg.) should provide plenty of offensive fireworks. Senior forwards 6-6 Kent Allison (13.1 ppg.-10.4 rpg.) and 6-5 Mike Odemns (9.7 ppg.-7.5 rpg.) will get the job done upfront. The Kentuckians could be set for a big year.

Location: Bowling Green, Ky. 42101
Enrollment: 11,750
Conference: Ohio Valley
Publicity: Ed Given
Office Phone: 502-745-4295

Nickname: Hilltoppers
Colors: Red & White
1973-74 Record: 15-10
Lettermen: Returning 9, Lost 1
Captain(s): TBA

Year by Year Scores

1942-43 Western 52-44	1964-65 La Salle 91-77
1947-48 Western 68-60	1965-66 Western 93-67
1949-50 La Salle 80-69	1966-67 Western 95-86
1950-51 Western 73-63	1967-68 Western 84-79
1951-52 La Salle 67-58	1968-69 La Salle 88-81
1956-57 Western 89-76	1969-70 Western 102-80
1958-59 La Salle 84-76	1970-71 La Salle 91-76
1958-59 Western 96-74	1971-72 Western 103-84
1959-60 Western 76-70	1972-73 La Salle 108-80
1960-61 Western 73-69	1973-74 La Salle 76-65
1961-62 La Salle 88-84	1973-74 Western .... 85-84 (OT)
1963-64 Western 107-95	

19. SYRACUSE UNIVERSITY

Saturday, February 1, 1975, 8:00 P.M., at the
Manley Field House, Syracuse, N.Y.

SERIES RECORD:
La Salle 14, Syracuse 10

Coach Roy Danforth
(Six Years, 105-53)

OUTLOOK: The Orange lost three starters, but are optimistic about attaining a fifth consecutive post-season tourney. The top returnees are senior co-captains 6-8 Rudy Hackett (16.8 ppg.-11.6 rpg.) and 6-2 Jim Lee (13.7 ppg.). 6-4 juniors Chris Sease (4.8 ppg.) and Kevin King (4.4 ppg.) were part-time regulars a year ago. Soph newcomers 6-9 Earnie Seibert (16.7 ppg.-14.0 rpg.-frosh), 6-9 Bob Parker (13.5 ppg.-12.9 rpg.-frosh) and 6-0 Larry Kelley (16.8 ppg.-frosh) are expected to have an impact. Among the better squads in the East once again!

Location: Syracuse, N.Y. 13210
Enrollment: 10,000
Conference: Independent
Publicity: Larry Kimball
Office Phone: 315-423-2608

Nickname: Orangemen
Colors: Orange
1973-74 Record: 19-7
Lettermen: Returning 9, Lost 6
Captain(s): Rudy Hackett & Jim Lee

Year by Year Scores

1954-55	La Salle	103-54	1964-65 Syracuse	104-81
1955-56	La Salle	75-62	1965-66 Syracuse	98-85
1955-56	La Salle	71-64	1966-67 Syracuse	88-84
1956-57	Syracuse	94-82	1966-67 Syracuse	102-81
1957-58	La Salle	59-55 (OT)	1967-68 La Salle	78-68
1958-59	La Salle	79-71	1967-68 La Salle	105-81
1959-60	Syracuse	91-84 (OT)	1968-69 La Salle	83-63
1960-61	La Salle	81-75	1969-70 La Salle	108-101
1961-62	La Salle	69-53	1970-71 Syracuse	75-68
1962-63	La Salle	74-66	1971-72 Syracuse	87-80
1963-64	La Salle	63-61	1972-73 Syracuse	91-84
1964-65	La Salle	73-70 (OT)	1973-74 Syracuse	75-68

20. DREXEL UNIVERSITY

Wednesday, February 5, 1975, 8:00 P.M., at the
Drexel Physical Education-Athletic Center, Philadelphia, Pa.

SERIES RECORD:
La Salle 5, Drexel 1

Coach Ray Haesler
(Three Years, 40-30)

OUTLOOK: Dragons can breathe fire on the front-line with capable returnees 6-5 junior Doug Romanczuk (9.3 ppg.-7.9 rpg.), 6-6 junior Mike Kernan (9.1 ppg.) and 6-4 senior Terry Parks (7.6 ppg.-6.4 rpg.). In addition, seniors 6-6 Doug White and 6-4 Tim Corlies should be recovered from injuries which hampered their play a year ago. 6-3 senior Mike Feagans (9.2 ppg.) will adequately fill one guard position but the other startingslot is a question mark. Lacking the 'big center' but with enough veteran strength to turn the corner.

Location: Philadelphia, Pa. 19104
Enrollment: 5,200
Conference: East Coast (East)
Publicity: Doug Verb
Office Phone: 215-895-2551

Nickname: Dragons
Colors: Blue & Gold
1973-74 Record: 15-9
Lettermen: Returning 9, Lost 5
Captain(s): Bob Ambler, Tim Corlies
& Terry Parks

Year by Year Scores

1944-45 La Salle 95-34	1971-72 Drexel 77-64
1944-45 La Salle 75-46	1972-73 La Salle 72-57
1970-71 La Salle 81-63	1973-74 La Salle 85-73

21. TEMPLE UNIVERSITY

Saturday, February 8, 1975, 9:15 P.M., at the Palestra, Philadelphia, Pa.

SERIES RECORD:
La Salle 28, Temple 34

OUTLOOK: A definite rebuilding prospectus for the Owls with senior co-captains 6-1 Kevin Washington (7.3 ppg.), the only holdover starter, and 6-7 George Bower (2.0 ppg.) in the leadership roles. Some September games in France this past fall should help! So will two frosh recruits, 6-7 Marvin Brown and 6-4 Tim Claxton, former Philadelphia scholastic standouts who might be starters. Newcomers will shape the season!

Coach Don Casey
(One Year, 16-9)

Location: Philadelphia, Pa. 19122
Enrollment: 16,397
Conference: East Coast (East)
Publicity: Al Shrier
Office Phone: 215-787-7445

Nickname: Owls
Colors: Cherry & White
1973-74 Record: 16-9
Lettermen: Returning 2, Lost 5
Captain(s): Kevin Washington &
George Bower

Year by Year Scores

1900-01 La Salle 15-10	1951-52 La Salle 75-59
1901-02 Temple 19-11	1951-52 La Salle 65-50
1902-03 Temple 16-14	1952-53 La Salle 57-42
1903-04 La Salle 20-13	1952-53 La Salle 65-45
1904-05 La Salle 19-17	1953-54 La Salle 77-53
1905-06 Temple 23-21	1953-54 Temple 57-56
1906-07 Temple 25-17	1954-55 La Salle 59-57
1907-08 Temple 29-20	1955-56 Temple 60-57
1908-09 La Salle 24-20	1956-57 La Salle 63-61
1909-10 Temple 29-18	1957-58 Temple 71-61
1910-11 Temple 30-21	1958-59 La Salle 67-64
1911-12 La Salle 35-16	1959-60 Temple 77-53
1912-13 Temple 27-22	1960-61 Temple 63-57
1913-14 Temple 28-19	1961-62 Temple 64-51
1914-15 Temple 37-21	1962-63 La Salle 81-71
1915-16 Temple 39-25	1963-64 Temple 63-57
1936-37 La Salle 37-31	1964-65 La Salle 83-70
1937-38 Temple 37-22	1964-65 La Salle 81-74
1938-39 La Salle 38-27	1965-66 Temple .... 66-59 (OT)
1939-40 Temple 39-37	1965-66 La Salle 86-85
1940-41 Temple 27-22	1966-67 Temple 79-65
1941-42 Temple 48-38	1966-67 Temple 78-61
1942-43 Temple 47-43	1967-68 La Salle 64-60
1943-44 Temple 73-45	1967-68 La Salle 87-69
1945-46 Temple 70-60	1968-69 La Salle 101-85
1946-47 La Salle 73-71	1969-70 Temple 69-61
1947-48 Temple 54-52	1970-71 La Salle 63-58
1948-49 Temple 54-36	1971-72 Temple 67-56
1949-50 La Salle 60-55	1972-73 Temple 56-54
1949-50 La Salle 67-51	1973-74 La Salle 78-54
1950-51 La Salle 82-65	
1950-51 Temple 59-54	

ALL TIME LA SALLE

Season	Won	Lost	Pts. For	Opp. Pts.	Coach
1974	18	10	2251	2029	Paul Westhead
1973	15	10	1885	1757	Paul Westhead
1972	6	19	1820	1957	Paul Westhead
1971	20	7	2065	1859	Paul Westhead
1970	14	12	2153	2048	Tom Gola
1969	23	1	2135	1702	Tom Gola
1968	20	8	2171	1924	Jim Harding
1967	14	12	2210	2111	Joe Heyer
1966	10	15	2136	2169	Joe Heyer
1965	15	8	1889	1737	Bob Walters
1964	16	9	1863	1786	Bob Walters
1963	16	8	1791	1606	Donald Moore
1962	16	9	1793	1674	Donald Moore
1961	15	7	1646	1522	Donald Moore
1960	16	6	1800	1700	Donald Moore
1959	16	7	1700	1676	Donald Moore
1958	16	9	1850	1803	Jim Pollard
1957	17	9	1972	1903	Jim Pollard
1956	15	10	1879	1716	Jim Pollard
1955	26	5	2503	1974	Ken Loeffler
1954	26	4	2261	1896	Ken Loeffler
1953	25	3	2243	1731	Ken Loeffler
1952	25	7	2376	2000	Ken Loeffler
1951	22	7	2089	1768	Ken Loeffler
1950	21	4	1646	1362	Ken Loeffler
1949	21	7	1758	1449	Charles McGlone
1948	20	4	1512	1236	Charles McGlone
1947	20	6	1507	1159	Charles McGlone
1946	9	14	1213	1334	Joseph Meehan
1945	12	7	1063	886	Joseph Meehan
1944	8	8	648	638	Joseph Meehan
1943	13	10	1044	966	"Obie" O'Brien
1942	12	11	997	919	"Obie" O'Brien
1941	9	8	770	714	Leonard Tanseer
1940	12	8	718	674	Leonard Tanseer
1939	12	6	689	603	Leonard Tanseer
1938	9	8	543	544	Leonard Tanseer
1937	12	8	629	531	Leonard Tanseer
1936	4	12	467	578	Leonard Tanseer
1935	16	6	668	517	Leonard Tanseer
1934	14	3	539	423	Leonard Tanseer
1933	13	3	492	399	Thomas Conley
1932	14	8	652	—	Thomas Conley
1931	15	4	551	—	James J. Henry

COACHING RECORDS

(Since 1931)

Coach	Years of Service	Won	Lost	Avg.
Paul Westhead	(4) 1970-74	59	46	.562
Tom Gola	(2) 1968-70	37	13	.740
Jim Harding	(1) 1967-68	20	8	.714
Joe Heyer	(2) 1965-67	24	27	.471
Bob Walters	(2) 1963-65	31	17	.646
Donald (Dudey) Moore	(5) 1959-63	79	37	.681
Jim Pollard	(3) 1956-58	48	28	.632
Kenneth Loeffler	(6) 1950-55	145	30	.829
Charles McGlone	(3) 1947-49	60	16	.789
Joseph Meehan	(3) 1944-46	29	29	.500
"Obie" O'Brien	(2) 1942-43	25	21	.577
Leonard Tanseer	(8) 1934-41	88	59	.598
Thomas Conley	(2) 1932-33	27	11	.711
James J. Henry	(1) 1930-31	15	4	.769
Totals	44 Years	687	346	.665

Name
Tom Gola ....
Ken Durrett ....
Hubie Marshall .
Larry Foust .....
Larry Cannon ...
Frank Corace ...
Norman Grekin .
Bernie Williams.

Name
Tom Gola ....
Tom Gola ....
Hubie Marshall
Ken Durrett .....
Bob Fields ....
Frank Corace ...
Ken Durrett .....
Bill Taylor .....
Hubie Marshall
Larry Cannon .
Bob McAteer ...
Tom Gola ....
Tom Gola ....
Jim Crawford .
Joe Bryant .....
Fran Dunphy ...
Ken Durrett .....

COLLEGE STATISTICS

Captain	Leading Scorer	Games	Field Goals	Foul Goals	Points
Joe DiCocco/Frank Moffatt	Bill Taylor	28	242	67	551
Jim Crawford/Bill Fox	Jim Crawford	25	175	139	489
Jim Crawford	Jim Crawford	25	147	100	394
Ken Durrett	Bob Fields	27	247	111	605
F. Dunphy/K. Durrett	Ken Durrett	26	249	134	632
Game Captains	Ken Durrett	24	191	98	480
L. Cannon/D. Ervin	Larry Cannon	28	207	132	546
H. Marshall/G. Paull	Hubie Marshall	26	220	109	549
Jerry Marano	Hubie Marshall	25	277	120	674
Joe Cunnane	Curt Fromal	23	182	77	441
Frank Corace	Frank Corace	25	242	117	601
B. Raftery/T. Abbott	Frank Corace	24	186	69	441
Bob McAteer	Bob McAteer	25	205	133	543
Bob McAteer	Bill Raftery	22	143	106	392
Game Captains	Bob Alden	22	122	116	360
Al Ferner	Joe Heyer	23	171	60	402
Chas. Eltringham	Bill Katheder	25	127	72	326
Game Captains	Al Lewis	26	165	129	459
Game Captains	Al Lewis	25	132	62	326
Tom Gola	Tom Gola	31	274	202	750
T. Gola/F. O'Hara	Tom Gola	30	252	186	690
Game Captains	Tom Gola	28	186	145	517
Charles Donnelly	Tom Gola	29	192	120	504
James Phelan	Jack George	29	200	69	469
Frank Comerford	Larry Foust	25	136	83	355
Joe Greenburg	Larry Foust	28	177	99	453
Joe Greenburg	Larry Foust	24	257	87	401
Fred Bernhardt	Bob Walters	23	—	—	348
Bob Walters	Bob Walters	23	160	47	367
Bob Walters	Bob Walters	17	108	31	247
Don Clune	Bob Walters	16	—	—	215
Irv Reichman					
Charles McGlone	Charles McGlone	23	79	24	182
G. Gillen/J. Brnich	Charles McGlone	17	85	18	188
Tom Carroll	Tom Carroll	20	67	18	152
Frank Hoerst	Frank Hoerst	18	66	42	174
Frank Hoerst	Frank Hoerst	17	53	27	130
Game Captains	Frank Hoerst	20	57	33	147
Phil Kear	Frank Hoerst	16	42	21	105
Matt Kratchowill	Clem Meehan	20	85	28	198
Clem Meehan	Charles Mosicant	17	34	48	116
Joe Meehan					
Charles Mosicant	Clem Meehan	22	63	32	158
Mort Gratz/Ray Bab	Mort Gratz	19	36	26	98

22. VILLANOVA UNIVERSITY

Wednesday, February 12, 1975, 9:15 P.M., at the Palestra, Philadelphia, Pa.

SERIES RECORD:
La Salle 12, Villanova 13

OUTLOOK: The Cats return four sophs in 6-8 Larry Herron (13.1 ppg.-7.3 rpg.), 6-2 Chubby Cox (11.8 ppg.), 6-7 John Olive (9.7 ppg.-6.5 rpg.) and 6-0 Joe Rogers (7.9 ppg.), all starters in '73-74. 6-6 senior Bob Sebastian (8.8 ppg.) and 6-4 junior Mike Stack, recovered from an injury, add quality depth. The Main Liners also have three talented frosh prospects, 6-6 Keith Herron, 6-6 Reggie Robinson and 6-4 Whitey Rigsby. A young club with great potential.

Coach Rollie Massimino
(One Year, 7-19)

Location: Villanova, Pa. 19085
Enrollment: 10,000
Conference: Independent
Publicity: TBA
Office Phone: 215-527-2100 Ext. 200

Nickname: Wildcats
Colors: Blue & White
1973-74 Record: 7-19
Lettermen: Returning 10, Lost 2
Captain(s): Jim Berrang, Ed Manning
& Bob Sebastian

Year by Year Scores

1933-34 Villanova 25-23	1962-63 Villanova 63-47
1934-35 Villanova 22-21	1963-64 La Salle 63-59
1934-35 La Salle 29-23	1964-65 Villanova 86-72
1955-56 Villanova 76-73	1965-66 La Salle 78-70
1955-56 La Salle 71-64	1966-67 Villanova 68-59
1956-57 La Salle 75-61	1967-68 Villanova 64-56
1957-58 La Salle ....111-105 (OT)	1968-69 La Salle 74-67
1957-58 La Salle 75-64	1969-70 Villanova 96-85
1958-59 Villanova 63-57	1970-71 La Salle 73-69
1959-60 Villanova 68-52	1971-72 Villanova 86-73
1960-61 La Salle 76-71	1972-73 La Salle 101-79
1961-62 Villanova 65-63	1973-74 La Salle 104-66
1961-62 Villanova 75-67	

La Salle COLLEGE

23. NOTRE DAME UNIVERSITY

Saturday, February 15, 1975, 2:00 P.M., at the Athletic and Convocation Center, Notre Dame, Indiana

SERIES RECORD:
La Salle 0, Notre Dame 3

Coach Richard Phelps
(Three Years, 50-35)

OUTLOOK: 6-5 soph Adrian Dantley (18.3 ppg.-9.7 rpg.) and 6-0 senior Dwight Clay (7.2 ppg.) are the only holdover starters from last year, but 6-5 soph Bill Paterno (7.7 ppg.) and 6-8 senior Pete Crotty add veteran talent. 6-9 soph Toby Knight and 6-1 soph Ray Martin will press for starting roles, and be challenged by frosh newcomers 6-8 Dave Batton and 6-3 Jeff Carpenter. Many coaches would love to have such a rebuilding prospectus.

Location: Notre Dame, Indiana 46556
Enrollment: 8,444
Conference: Independent
Publicity: Roger O. Valdiserri
Office Phone: 219-283-7516

Nickname: Fighting Irish
Colors: Blue & Gold
1973-74 Record: 26-3
Lettermen: Returning 8, Lost 3
Captain(s): TBA

Year by Year Scores

1971-72 Notre Dame 97-71
1972-73 Notre Dame 87-71
1973-74 Notre Dame 98-78

24. AMERICAN UNIVERSITY

Wednesday, February 19, 1975, 8:00 P.M., at the Ft. Myer Arena, Arlington, Va.

SERIES RECORD:
La Salle 8, American 2

Coach Jim Lynam
(One Year, 16-10)

OUTLOOK: The loss of four graduated starters is soothed somewhat by the return of 6-7 senior Wilbur Thomas (18.3 ppg.-10.4 rpg.). Best bets to crack into the frontcourt lineup are 6-7 senior Bill Mann (4.4 ppg.), 6-5 soph Calvin Brown (5.0 ppg.) and 6-6 transfer Ricky Hunt. Sophs 6-0 Dante Fulton (20.6 ppg.-JV) and 6-5 Cleo Wright (19.8 ppg.-JV) could be the starting guards, but frosh newcomers 6-1 Howie Kane and 6-0 Donald Kelly figure to challenge. Rebuilding, but using top-notch young talent to do it.

Location: Washington, D.C. 20016
Enrollment: 5,000
Conference: East Coast (East)
Publicity: Ray Murphy
Office Phone: 202-686-2560

Nickname: Eagles
Colors: Red, White & Blue
1973-74 Record: 16-10
Lettermen: Returning 5, Lost 5
Captain(s):

Year by Year Scores

1965-66 La Salle 103-93		1969-70 La Salle 106-86
1966-67 American ...... 94-90 (OT)		1970-71 La Salle 62-54
1967-68 La Salle 74-65		1971-72 La Salle 59-53
1967-68 La Salle 84-57		1972-73 American 88-79
1968-69 La Salle 96-72		1973-74 La Salle 95-83

25. RUTGERS UNIVERSITY

Saturday, February 22, 1975, 7:15 P.M., at the Palestra, Philadelphia, Pa.

SERIES RECORD:
La Salle 2, Rutgers 0

OUTLOOK: 6-5 junior Phil Sellers (23.2 ppg.-9.3 rpg.) and 6-4 junior Mike Dabney (15.8 ppg.-6-9 rpg.) head a long list of returning vets. 6-1 soph Ed Jordan (11.1 ppg.) is a fixture at a guard spot, and 6-10 soph Les Cason was occasionally brilliant in the pivot last season. 6-6 frosh Hollis Copeland is a blue chip addition. The Scarlet Knights will enter elite Eastern circles.

Coach Tom Young
(One Year, 18-8)

Location: New Brunswick, N.J. 08902
Enrollment: 16,000
Conference: Independent
Publicity: Robert Currie
Office Phone: 201-932-7315

Nickname: Scarlet Knights
Colors: Scarlet
1973-74 Record: 18-8
Lettermen: Returning 12, Lost 1
Captain(s): TBA

Year by Year Scores

1960-61 La Salle 85-63
1973-74 La Salle 82-76

6-7 All-American Ken Durrett (no. 33) lefthands two of his 45 points which sparked La Salle's 91-76 rout of Western Kentucky and set new Palestra and Explorers' standards during the 1970-71 campaign. Durrett, MAC and Big Five MVP, finished his career with 1679 points, second highest total in La Salle history. Ken's career per-game average of 23.6 is the school's best ever.

THE EXPLORERS' 1973-74 SEASON IN REVIEW

This season was a mixture of joy and frustration. I know, however,
that we gave every effort. Our goals for the future are filled with
great hope and determination.

(Paul Westhead, La Salle Basketball Coach)

La Salle basketball continued an upward trend in 1973-74. Coach Paul Westhead's
Explorer squad had a good year! They missed having a 'very good year' by the
narrowest of margins.

This past season La Salle registered 18 victories, a win-total topped by only three
other Explorer teams in the past 15 years.

La Salle's ultimate quest for the Middle Atlantic Conference title fell short by only
five points, a 76-71 loss to St. Joseph's. They missed the coveted Big Five championship by four points, an 84-82 defeat by Penn, and a 75-73 loss to St. Joe's. The
Explorers lost at Western Kentucky and Duquesne, but so did Providence, the East's
best team.

La Salle did finish a strong third in both New York's ECAC Holiday Festival and
St. Petersburg, Florida's Big Sun Invitational.

A sampling of their '73-74 victims is impressive! Rutgers, Stanford, Princeton,
Western Kentucky, Niagara, Holy Cross, American, Temple and Villanova were each
defeated by the Explorers.

And in the process, La Salle's Bill Taylor emerged as one of the East's premiere
players. The 6-5 junior from Tuskegee, Alabama, notched 551 points this year, the
eighth best single season-total in Explorer history.

Taylor's 19.7 ppg. scoring average was the highest in both the MAC and the Big
Five. 'B.T.' was over 20 points on 11 different occasions, highlighted by a 39 point
explosion vs. American University, when he canned 18 of 22 field goal attempts.

In other outstanding efforts, Taylor scored 28 points vs. St. Joseph's and Lafayette,
27 points vs. Wake Forest, 26 points vs. Holy Cross, and 25 points vs. Notre Dame
and Princeton.

The debut of Philadelphia's 6-10 soph Joe Bryant proved to be almost as explosive.
'J.B.' scored 486 points and pulled down 282 rebounds in a rookie performance
topped by only one previous La Salle player (Tom Gola had 504 points and 497
rebounds as a frosh in '51-52).

Bryant's 18.7 ppg. gave him second place in the Big Five and MAC scoring races,
and his 10.8 rpg. showing off the boards led the Big Five and was the MAC's
second-best.

Joe's high '73-74 outputs were 37 points against Rider and 17 rebounds against
Delaware in the MAC playoffs.

Joining Taylor and Bryant on the frontline was 6-6 senior Joe DiCocco, a hard-
nosed boardman from Upper Darby, Pa., who started all 78 games in his varsity
career. Joe's three year totals of 847 points and 741 rebounds attest to his steady
and solid play. For '73-74, he averaged 10.5 ppg. and 9.4 rpg., with best efforts of
21 points vs. Stanford, and 16 rebounds vs. Syracuse.

The Explorer backcourt featured all kinds of depth. While sophomores Glenn Collier
and Charlie Wise got the starting nods, seniors Steve Baruffi and Frank Moffatt saw
plenty of action.

The 6-2 Collier from Philadelphia emerged as a smooth playmaker with a soft
touch, averaging 7.3 ppg., passing off for 97 assists and hitting a career-high 18
points vs. Lafayette.

Known for his defensive prowess, 6-0 'Sweet Charlie' Wise from Cape May, New
Jersey, was the eighth best scorer in the Big Five with 11.9 ppg., and finished second
in assists with 110. Wise got a career-high 19 points vs. Stanford, Western Kentucky
and Delaware.

Baruffi, a 6-1 flash from Vineland, New Jersey, proved to be a regularly-spectacular
sixth man, adding a solid 5.8 ppg. off the bench throughout 1973-74. Called upon
to start in the absence of the injured Joe Bryant, Steve burned American University
with a first class 20 point outburst.

Moffatt, the 5-10 'mighty mite' from Cherry Hill, New Jersey, was the proof positive that the little man still has a place in collegiate basketball. Frank frequently
gave Wise and Collier a breather, running the attack with precision and cleverness,
and throwing the key pass. Moffatt averaged 3.1 ppg., topped by 11 points vs. Notre
Dame, and fed 48 assists in his spot duty.

And the list of contributors goes on! Seniors Frank 'Cat' Doyle and Joe 'Rabbi'
Rapczynski, honored by the Philadelphia sportswriters as La Salle's 'unsung heroes',
junior Kevin McBain, sophomore Varick Cutler, and freshmen Donn Wilber and Barry
Brodzinski, added time and talent to the success of the Explorer unit.

In summation, 1973-74 La Salle basketball was exciting, competitive and representative! It was not a 'very good year', because the Explorers did not win the NCAA
berth! However, it was indeed a good year! La Salle earned and deserved a bid to the
National Invitational Tournament.

1973-74 EXPLORER HIGH MARKS

INDIVIDUAL

POINTS SCORED (GAME)—39, Bill Taylor vs. American
POINTS SCORED (HALF)—23, Bill Taylor vs. American
REBOUNDS—17, Joe Bryant vs. Delaware
FIELD GOALS—18, Bill Taylor vs. American (22 attempts)
FREE THROWS—10, Joe Bryant vs. Holy Cross (12 attempts)
ASSISTS—11, Glenn Collier vs. Lafayette

TEAM

POINTS SCORED (GAME)—104, vs. Villanova
POINTS SCORED (HALF)—61, vs. Villanova
REBOUNDS—55, vs. Villanova
FIELD GOALS—47, vs. Biscayne (74 attempts)
FREE THROWS—26, vs. Holy Cross (32 attempts)
ASSISTS—24, vs. Holy Cross

1973-74 ATTENDANCE

La Salle's basketball squad played before a total of 125,607 fans during the '73-74 campaign for an average of 4485.

The Explorer's attracted 57,755 spectators in 14 road shows (over 9500 miles) for an average of 4125, and 67,852 court followers in 14 home battles for an average of 4846.

The La Salle five's largest home crowd was a 9,222 Palestra sellout vs. Notre Dame, while the Explorers' top road draw was 9,100 at Western Kentucky.

TOP INDIVIDUAL OPPONENT PERFORMANCES, 1973-74

PLAYER (TEAM)	EFFORT	GAME OUTCOME
Gary Brokaw (Notre Dame)	28 pts. (10-14, 8-11), 6 asst.*	98-78, Notre Dame
†Phil Sellers (Rutgers)	28 pts. (13-21, 2-2), 10 rbs.*	82-76, La Salle
†Wilbur Thomas (American)	27 pts. (10-20, 7-9), 7 rbs.	95-83, La Salle
Dave Frost (Stanford)	26 pts. (9-20, 8-10), 8 rbs.	77-66, La Salle
Malcolm Moulton (Holy Cross)	25 pts. (9-15, 7-11), 7 rbs.	94-80, La Salle
Andy Rimol (Princeton)	24 pts. (11-16, 2-2), 6 rbs.	83-78, La Salle
†Andy Walker (Niagara)	23 pts. (11-21, 1-1), 14 rbs.	67-65, La Salle
†Rudy Hackett (Syracuse)	20 pts. (8-18, 4-4), 22 rbs.*	75-68, Syracuse
Jim O'Brien (St. Joseph's)	19 pts. (4-7, 11-12), 10 asst.*	76-71, St. Joseph's

*1973-74 Opponent High   †Player to face La Salle in 1974-75

1973-74 SEASON RESULTS AND
GAME-BY-GAME SCORING

OPPONENT	LSC SCORE	OPP. SCORE	Bryant	Taylor	DiCocco	Wise	Baruffi	Collier	Moffatt	McBain	Doyle	Wilber	Brodzinski	Rapczynski	Cutler
	87	37	19	15	14	8	4	3	8	4	6	4	0	2	—
												0	—	—	—	0
												1	—	0	—	—
H) Niagara	67	65	26	12	17	8	0	4	0	—	—	—	—	—	0
(A) W. Kentucky	84	85	15	24	11	19	4	6	5	—	0	—	—	—	—
(H) Drexel	85	73	17	16	15	11	8	8	6	0	2	—	2	0	0
(H) Lafayette	87	66	14	28	6	8	9	18	2	2	0	—	—	0	—
(A) Biscayne	97	75	15	24	8	13	1	10	4	12	4	—	0	2	4
(A) Canisius	81	89	26	24	8	14	6	6	0	0	—	—	—	—	—
(H) St. Joseph's	73	75	21	28	8	2	0	10	3	1	0	—	—	—	—
(H) Temple	78	54	22	18	8	9	2	12	0	1	0	0	0	6	0
(H) Notre Dame	78	98	6	25	10	14	4	3	11	4	0	—	0	1	—
(H) American	95	83	—	39	10	10	20	6	6	2	0	0	0	0	2
(A) West Chester	73	53	—	16	8	12	8	6	5	6	4	2	2	2	2
(A) Duquesne	63	81	14	17	4	14	4	4	2	4	0	—	0	—	—
(H) Villanova	104	66	15	21	16	10	6	9	6	—	4	9	2	4	2
(A) Rutgers	82	76	16	17	14	13	8	12	2	—	—	—	—	—	—
(H) Delaware*†	78	69	14	16	4	19	6	15	4	0	—	—	0	—	—
(H) Rider*†	84	68	37	22	4	7	6	4	4	0	0	—	—	0	—
(H) St. Joseph's*†	71	76	20	20	4	15	0	10	2	—	—	—	—	—	—

(H) Home; (A) Away; (*) Big Sun Tourney at St. Petersburg, Fla.; (†) ECAC Holiday Festival at New York; (*†) MAC Playoffs at Philadelphia

39

1973-74 TWENTY-EIGHT GAME LA SALLE COLLEGE BASKETBALL STATS

PLAYER	G	FG	FGA	PCT	FT	FTA	PCT	SM	RBS	AVG	A	PF-D	PTS	AVG
Taylor, Bill	28	242	502	48.2	67	101	66.3	294	197	7.0	57	72-2	551	19.7
Bryant, Joe	26	200	440	45.4	86	123	69.9	277	282	10.8	30	72-3	486	18.7
Wise, Charlie	28	148	289	51.2	39	56	69.6	158	80	2.8	110	86-4	335	11.9
DiCocco, Joe	28	124	286	43.3	46	67	68.7	183	263	9.4	58	90-5	294	10.5
Collier, Glenn	28	94	180	52.2	16	28	57.1	98	60	2.1	97	80-4	204	7.3
Baruffi, Steve	28	67	140	47.8	28	45	62.2	90	65	2.3	37	66-2	162	5.8
Moffatt, Frank	28	32	60	53.3	22	23	95.7	29	21	0.7	48	49-2	86	3.1
Wilber, Donn	7	6	11	54.5	6	9	66.7	8	8	1.1	0	8-0	18	2.6
McBain, Kevin	22	25	54	46.2	6	11	54.5	34	47	2.1	5	21-1	56	2.5
Doyle, Frank	15	8	20	40.0	6	8	75.0	14	13	0.8	2	11-0	22	1.5
Rapczynski, Joe	12	6	15	40.0	5	7	71.4	11	12	1.0	2	4-0	17	1.4
Cutler, Varick	9	5	9	55.6	2	2	100.0	4	13	1.4	0	4-0	12	1.3
Brodzinski, Barry	11	3	11	27.3	2	3	66.7	9	8	0.7	7	2-0	8	0.7

TEAM REBOUNDS—154

	G	FG	FGA	PCT	FT	FTA	PCT	SM	RBS	AVG	A	PF-D	PTS	AVG
LSC TOTALS	28	960	2017	47.6	331	483	68.5	1209	1223	43.7	453	565-23	2251	80.4
OPP TOTALS	28	831	1864	44.6	367	528	69.5	1194	1180	42.1	439	466-16	2029	72.4

SEASON RESULTS

(Won 18, Lost 10)

OPPONENT	LSC	OPP
Lehigh (H)	87	37
Army (A)	83	71
Hofstra (A)	66	53
Syracuse (H)	68	75-
Holy Cross (A)	94	80
Pennsylvania (H)	82	84-
Wake Forest*	90	95-
Western Kentucky*	76	65
Stanford**	77	66
Manhattan**	65	73-
Princeton**	83	78
Niagara (H)	67	65
Western Kentucky (A)	84	85-(OT)
Drexel (H)	85	73
Lafayette (H)	87	66
Biscayne (A)	97	75
Canisius (A)	81	89-
St. Joseph's (H)	73	75-
Temple (H)	78	54
Notre Dame (H)	78	98-
American (H)	95	83
West Chester (A)	73	53
Duquesne (A)	63	81-
Villanova	104	66
Rutgers (A)	82	76
Delaware†	78	69
Rider†	84	68
St. Joseph's†	71	76-

* Big Sun Tourney, St. Petersburg, Fla.
** Holiday Festival, New York
† MAC Playoffs at the Palestra

FINAL 1973-74 BIG FIVE STANDINGS

	CONFERENCE			ALL GAMES		
TEAM	W	L	PCT.	W	L	PCT.
Pennsylvania	4	0	1.000	21	6	.778
La Salle	2	2	.500	18	10	.643
St. Joseph's	2	2	.500	19	11	.633
Temple	2	2	.500	16	9	.640
Villanova	0	4	.000	7	19	.269

LA SALLE AND 11 OTHERS DISSOLVE MAC TIES, FORM EAST COAST CONFERENCE

The East Coast Conference, composed of 12 former Middle Atlantic Conference University Division members including La Salle, is in its first year of athletic competition, having begun formal operation July 1, 1974.

The athletic alliance has as charter members American University, Bucknell University, the University of Delaware, Drexel University, Hofstra University, Lafayette College, La Salle College, Lehigh University, Rider College, St. Joseph's College, Temple University, and West Chester State College.

All twelve schools are members of the Eastern Collegiate Athletic Conference (ECAC) and are listed as division one by the National Collegiate Athletic Association (NCAA). Gettysburg College, also a former member of the MAC's university division, decided against division one status and remained a member of the Middle Atlantic Conference. There will be East and West division competition in all team sports with conference champions moving on to NCAA competition.

East division members include American, Drexel, Hofstra, La Salle, St. Joseph's, and Temple. The West will have Bucknell, Delaware, Lafayette, Lehigh, Rider, and West Chester.

However, since most schedules for the 1974-75 athletic calendar have already been drawn, West Chester will be a member of the East division for one year, before shifting to the West for the 1975-76 school year.

Bucknell Athletic Director Rober A. Latour has been elected president of the new league with La Salle's John J. Conboy serving as vice president, and Rider's John B. Carpenter as secretary-treasurer. Temple's Ernest C. Casale has been chosen league commissioner and Michael Trilling will be the conference publicity director.

FINAL MIDDLE ATLANTIC CONFERENCE UNIVERSITY DIVISION

BASKETBALL STANDINGS
1973-74

EASTERN SECTION

	League			Points		Overall			Points	
	W	L	Pct	F	A	W	L	Pct	F	A
*St. Joseph's	5	1	833	444	364	19	10	655	1970	1820
La Salle	5	1	833	470	391	18	10	643	2251	2029
American	4	2	667	382	380	16	10	615	1829	1800
Temple	4	2	667	400	375	16	9	640	1503	1417
Drexel	2	4	333	401	443	15	9	625	1614	1501
Hofstra	1	5	167	395	480	8	16	333	1652	1865
West Chester	0	6	000	336	415	11	15	423	1688	1759

WESTERN SECTION

Rider	8	2	800	591	581	13	13	500	1592	1610
Lafayette	7	3	700	730	641	17	9	654	1851	1697
Delaware	7	3	700	711	630	15	11	577	1889	1827
Gettysburg	4	6	400	668	664	15	10	600	1796	1710
Bucknell	2	8	200	611	686	8	16	333	1518	1665
Lehigh	2	8	200	621	730	3	21	125	1406	1780

MAC PLAYOFFS

Quarterfinals
Lafayette 59, American 55
La Salle 78, Delaware 69

Semifinals
St. Joseph's 64, Lafayette 61 (OT)
La Salle 84, Rider 68

Finals
St. Joseph's 76, La Salle 71

ALL-TIME LA SALLE RECORDS
INDIVIDUAL RECORDS

LSC—one game:

POINTS:
45, Ken Durrett, vs. Western Kentucky, January 16, 1971.
FIELD GOALS ATTEMPTED:
33, Tom Gola, vs. Temple, February 26, 1955.
33, Frank Corace, vs. Penn, February 12, 1963.
33, Hubie Marshall, vs. Penn, December 21, 1966.
FIELD GOALS MADE:
20, Bob McAteer (28 atts.), vs. Millersville, December 1, 1961.
20, Ken Durrett (27 atts.), vs. Lafayette, February 4, 1970.
FREE THROWS ATTEMPTED:
21, Bob Fields, vs. Rider, March 1, 1971.
FREE THROWS MADE:
17 (18 atts.), Bob McAteer, vs. W. Kentucky, March 2, 1962.
REBOUNDS:
37, Tom Gola, vs. Lebanon Valley, January 15, 1955.
POINTS IN ONE-HALF:
33, Hubie Marshall, vs. Albright, December 1, 1965.

LSC—one season:

POINTS:
750, Tom Gola, 1954-55.
FIELD GOALS:
277, Hubie Marshall, 1965-66.
FREE THROWS ATTEMPTED:
267, Tom Gola, 1954-55.
FREE THROWS MADE:
202, Tom Gola, 1954-55.

Opponents—one game:

HUBIE MARSHALL

POINTS:
52, Calvin Murphy, Niagara, December 16, 1967.
FIELD GOALS ATTEMPTED:
40, Joe Steiner, Bucknell, February 7, 1962.
FIELD GOALS MADE:
20, Joe Steiner, Bucknell, February 7, 1962.
FREE THROWS ATTEMPTED:
23, Howie Landa, Lebanon Valley, January 15, 1955.
FREE THROWS MADE:
18, Bob McNeill, St. Joseph's, February 26, 1958.
Dariel Carrier, W. Kentucky, February 25, 1964.
REBOUNDS:
33, Art Beatty, American U., January 10, 1967.

TEAM RECORDS

LSC—one game:

COMBINED SCORE:
220 (99-121), vs. Miami, Fla., January 23, 1964.
POINTS:
125, vs. Loyola (La.), February 4, 1967.
LARGEST VICTORY MARGIN:
75 (LSC 95, P.M.C. 20), vs. P.M.C., January 29, 1947.

BOB McATEER

42

FIELD GOALS ATTEMPTED:
  112, vs. Furman, February 6, 1954.
FIELD GOALS:
  56, vs. Loyola (La.), February 4, 1967.
FREE THROWS TRIED:
  51, vs. Duquesne, February 16, 1957.
FREE THROWS MADE:
  36, vs. Pennsylvania, January 22, 1969.
REBOUNDS:
  85, vs. Brandeis and Canisius (1955).
ASSISTS:
  35, vs. Loyola (La.), February 4, 1967.
POINTS ONE-HALF:
  67, vs. St. Francis (Pa.), January 28, 1969.
PERSONAL FOULS:
  34, vs. Biscayne, February 15, 1972

Opponents—one game:
MOST POINTS:
  121, Miami, Fla., January 23, 1964.
FIELD GOALS ATTEMPTED:
  105, Creighton, February 1, 1967.
FIELD GOALS MADE:
  47, Miami, Fla., January 23, 1964.
FREE THROWS ATTEMPTED:
  52, N.C. State, January 23, 1954.
FREE THROWS MADE:
  37, Valparaiso, December 29, 1956.
  37, W. Kentucky, February 25, 1964.
REBOUNDS:
  79, St. Joseph's, January 8, 1966.

LSC—one season:
POINTS:
  2,503 in 31 games, 1954-55.
POINTS-PER-GAME:
  89.0 in 24 games, 1968-69.
FIELD GOALS MADE:
  959 in 31 games, 1954-55.
FREE THROWS ATTEMPTED:
  879 in 28 games, 1952-53.
FREE THROWS MADE:
  585 in 31 games, 1954-55.

Other Team Records:
MOST VICTORIES:
  26, 1953-54 and 1954-55.
MOST LOSSES:
  19, 1971-72.
LONGEST WINNING STREAK:
  15 games (1968-69).
BEST SEASON RECORD:
  W 23, L 1 (1968-69).

LARRY FOUST

FRANK CORACE

TOM GOLA

TOURNAMENT RECORDS

MID-SEASON

	Won	Lost	Pct.	Champions	Runners-up
Charlotte Invitational	2	0	1.000	1970	
Richmond Invitational	2	0	1.000	1958	
Quaker City Tourney	17	7	.708	1964, 69	1968, 72
Orange Bowl Tourney	2	1	.667		
ECAC Holiday Festival	15	9	.625		1955
Kentucky Invitation	2	2	.500		1954, 55
Boston Garden Tourney	1	1	.500		
Vanderbilt Invitational	1	1	.500		1967
Volunteer Classic	1	1	.500		1969
'Husker Classic	1	1	.500		1971
Sunshine Classic	1	1	.500		
Cable Car Classic	0	2	.000		
Totals	45	26	.634	4	8

1952-53 Holiday Festival, New York (5th Place)
De Paul 63 ....La Salle 61
La Salle 86 ....Cincinnati 81
La Salle 80 ....New York U. 63

1953-54 Kentucky Invitational (2nd Place)
La Salle 62 ....UCLA 53
Kentucky 73 ....La Salle 60

1953-54 Holiday Festival, New York (3rd Place)
La Salle 77 ....St. Louis 63
Niagara 69 ....La Salle 50
La Salle 74 ....Brigham Young 62

1954-55 Kentucky Invitational (2nd Place)
La Salle 49 ....S. California 38
Kentucky 63 ....La Salle 54

1954-55 Holiday Festival, New York (2nd Place)
La Salle 103 ....Syracuse 54
La Salle 85 ....UCLA 77
Duquesne 67 ....La Salle 65

1955-56 Holiday Festival, New York (5th Place)
San Francisco 79 ....La Salle 62
La Salle 75 ....Syracuse 72
La Salle 85 ....St. John's 76

1956-57 Orange Bowl Tournament, Miami Beach, Fla. (5th Place)
W. Kentucky 89 ....La Salle 76
La Salle 82 ....Seton Hall 72
La Salle 103 ....Valparaiso 73

1957-58 Richmond (Va.) Invitational (Won Championship)
La Salle 72 ....Virginia 64
La Salle 59 ....(OT)..........................Richmond 55

1961-62 Holiday Festival, New York (4th Place)
La Salle 87 ....Dartmouth 60
Cincinnati 64 ....La Salle 56
Dayton 81 ....La Salle 67

1962-63 Quaker City Festival, Palestra (5th Place)

Brigham Young 84 ....La Salle 73
La Salle 80 ....Delaware 64
La Salle 74 ....(OT)..................Bowling Green 67

1963-64 Quaker City Festival, Palestra (Won Championship)

La Salle 91 ....Northwestern 69
La Salle 80 ....Georgetown 69
La Salle 83 ....St. Bonaventure 80

1964-65 Holiday Festival, New York (5th Place)

St. John's 78 ....La Salle 71
La Salle 83 ....Temple 70
La Salle 73 ....(OT).....................Syracuse 70

1965-66 Quaker City Festival, Palestra (4th Place)

La Salle 71 ....Brigham Young 69
Temple 66 ....(OT)....................La· Salle 59
Minnesota 92 ....La Salle 87

1966-67 Vanderbilt Invitational, Nashville (2nd Place)

La Salle 99 ....Nebraska 76
Vanderbilt 100 ....La Salle 95

1966-67 Quaker City Festival, Palestra (5th Place)

Syracuse 88 ....La Salle 84
La Salle 86 ....Niagara 72
La Salle 78 ....Bowling Green 77

1967-68 Boston Garden Christmas Tournament (3rd Place)

Providence 77 ....La Salle 56
La Salle 68 ....North Carolina St. 63

1967-68 Holiday Festival, New York (5th Place)

Louisville 94 ....La Salle 71
La Salle 100 ....West Virginia 83
La Salle 78 ....Syracuse 68

1968-69 Quaker City Festival, Spectrum (2nd Place)

La Salle 70 ....Penn State 55
La Salle 108 ....Indiana 88
South Carolina 62 ....La Salle 59

1969-70 Volunteer Classic, Knoxville, Tenn. (2nd Place)

La Salle 81 ....Yale 59
La Salle 47 ....Tennessee 55

1969-70 Quaker City Festival, Palestra (Champions)

La Salle 76 ....Georgia 66
La Salle 68 ....Cornell 56
La Salle 89 ....Columbia 74

1970-71 Charlotte Invitational (Champions)

La Salle 50 ....Georgia 42
La Salle 75 ....Boston College 63

1971-72 Cornhusker Classic, Lincoln, Neb. (2nd Place)

La Salle 81 ....Baylor 68
Nebraska 75 ....La Salle 60

1971-72 Quaker City Festival, Palestra (5th Place)

Boston College 62 ....La Salle 61
La Salle 108 ....Fairfield 96
La Salle 82 ....Massachusetts 75

1972-73 Cable Car Classic, San Francisco, Cal.

USF 74 ....La Salle 73
Santa Clara 71 .... La Salle 69 (ovt.)

1972-73 Quaker City Festival, Palestra (2nd place)

La Salle 77 ....USC 72
La Salle 76 .... N. Mexico State 70
St. Joseph's 77 ....La Salle 52

1973-74 Sunshine Classic, **St.** Petersburg, **Fla. (3rd place)**
      Wake Forest 95 ....La Salle 90
      La Salle 76 ....W. Kentucky 65

1973-74 Holiday Festival, New York (3rd place)
      La Salle 77 ....Stanford 66
      Manhattan 73 .... La Salle 65
      La Salle 83 ....Princeton 78

POST-SEASON

	Won	Lost	Pct.	Champions	Runners-up
N.C.A.A.	9	2	.818	1954	1955
Nationai Invitational Tourney (NIT)	5	7	.417	1952	
Totals	14	9	.609	2	1

NCAA TOURNAMENT

1954 (**Won National** Championship)
      La Salle 76 ....(OT).........................Fordham 74
      La Salle 88 ....N. Carolina St. 81
      La Salle 64 ....Navy 48
      La Salle 69 ....Penn State 54
      La Salle 92 ....Bradley 76

1955 (Eastern Champions and National Runners-up)
      La Salle 95 ....W. Virginia 61
      La Salle 73 ....Princeton 46
      La Salle 99 ....Canisius 64
      La Salle 76 ....Iowa 73
      San Francisco 77 ....La Salle 63

1968 (Eliminated in First Round)
      Columbia 83 ....La Salle 69

NATIONAL INVITATIONAL TOURNEY (NIT)

1948 (Eliminated in First Round)
      Wèstern Kentucky 68 ....La Salle 61

1950 (Reached Quarter-Finals)
      La Salle 72 ....Arizona 66
      Duquesne 49 ....La Salle 47

1951 (Eliminated in First Round)
      St. Louis 73 ....La Salle 61

1952 (Won Championship)
      La Salle 80 ....Seton Hall 76
      La Salle 51 ....St. John's 45
      La Salle 59 ....Duquesne 46
      La Salle 75 ....Dayton 64

1953 (Seeded in Quarter-Finals)
      St. John's 75 ....La Salle 74

1963 (Eliminated in First Round)
      St. Louis 62 ....La Salle 61

1965 (Eliminated in First Round)
      Detroit 93 ....La Salle 86

1971 (Eliminated in First Round)
      Georgia Tech 70 ....La Salle 67

EXPLORER CENTURY MARKS (39)

(Opponents have scored **100** against **La** Salle **19** times)

YEAR	RESULT	SITE
1973-74	LA SALLE 104, Villanova 69	Palestra
1972-73	LA SALLE 101, Villanova 79	Palestra
1972-73	LA SALLE 108, W. Kentucky 80	Palestra
1971-72	LA SALLE 108, Fairfield 96	Palestra
1969-70	LA SALLE 108, Syracuse 101	Palestra
1969-70	LA SALLE 106, American 86	Palestra
1969-70	LA SALLE 102, Lafayette 73	Palestra
1969-70	LA SALLE 101, Niagara 90	Palestra
1968-69	LA SALLE 100, Baltimore 57	Palestra
1968-69	LA SALLE 108, Indiana 88	Spectrum
1968-69	LA SALLE 103, Creighton 84	Palestra
1968-69	LA SALLE 101, Temple 85	Palestra
1968-69	LA SALLE 107, St. Francis (Pa.) 95	Altoona, Pa.
1968-69	LA SALLE 102, Loyola (South) 65	Palestra
1967-68	LA SALLE 100, W. Virginia 83	Madison Sq. Garden
1967-68	LA SALLE 103, St. Joseph's 71	Palestra
1967-68	LA SALLE 105, Syracuse 81	Palestra
1966-67	LA SALLE 103, Gettysburg 67	Palestra
1966-67	LA SALLE 125, Loyola (La.) 80	Palestra
1966-67	LA SALLE 108, Oklahoma City 97	Palestra
1965-66	LA SALLE 103, American U. 93	Palestra
1965-66	LA SALLE 102, Miami 108	Miami, Fla.
1964-65	LA SALLE 101, Seton Hall 71	Palestra
1963-64	LA SALLE 100, Lafayette 86	Palestra
1962-63	LA SALLE 105, Bucknell 55	Palestra
1961-62	LA SALLE 102, Millersville 62	Lincoln High
1960-61	LA SALLE 104, Lafayette 86	Easton, Pa.
1958-59	LA SALLE 102, Georgetown 72	Washington, D.C.
1957-58	*LA SALLE 111, Villanova 105	Palestra
1956-57	LA SALLE 103, Valparaiso 73	Miami Beach, Fla.
1954-55	LA SALLE 103, Syracuse 54	Madison Sq. Garden
1954-55	LA SALLE 102, Brandeis 56	Convention Hall
1954-55	LA SALLE 112, Lebanon Valley 70	Convention Hall
1953-54	LA SALLE 100, Furman 83	Convention Hall
1952-53	LA SALLE 101, Albright 62	Reading, Pa.
1952-53	LA SALLE 111, West Chester 60	La Salle Fieldhouse
1952-53	LA SALLE 106, Muhlenberg 73	La Salle Fieldhouse
1951-52	LA SALLE 103, Geneva 74	Beaver Falls, Pa.
1951-52	LA SALLE 105, Murray State 82	Convention Hall

*Triple Overtime (1st team ever to score 100 against La Salle)

ALL-TIME RECORD WITH COLLEGIATE OPPONENTS

(Bold Face Name: 1974-75 Opponents)

Opponent	Won	Lost	First Met	Last Met	Last La Salle Victory	Last Opp. Victory
Akron	1	0	1940	1940	1940 (33-30)	
Alabama					(First Meeting)	
Albright	26	2	1946	1970	1970 (89-59)	1946 (67-61)
Alumni	12	0	1931	1948	1948 (71-35)	
American U.	8	2	**1966**	**1974**	**1974(95-83)**	**1973(88-79)**
Arizona	2	0	1950	1953	1953 (87-68)	
Arkansas	1	0	1948	1948	1948 (69-58)	
Army	2	0	**1973**	**1974**	**1974(83-71)**	
Arnold	1	0	1943	1943	1943 (83-48)	
Baldwin-Wallace	2	1	1949	1951	1951 (86-67)	1949 (52-49)
Baltimore U.	4	0	1933	1969	1969 (100-57)	
Baylor	1	0	1972	1972	1972 (81-68)	
Biscayne	2	1	**1972**	**1974**	**1974(97-75)**	**1972(103-93)**
Bloomsburg	1	0	1950	1950	1950 (67-41)	
Boston College	3	1	1947	1972	1971 (75-63)	1972 (62-61)
Bowling Green	4	1	1949	1967	1967 (78-77)	1949 (51-45)
Bradley	2	1	1954	1957	1957 (87-77)	1956 (93-78)
Brandeis	1	0	1955	1955	1955 (102-56)	
Brigham Young	3	1	1949	1966	1966 (71-69)	1963 (84-73)
Brooklyn College	1	0	1935	1935	1935 (28-17)	
Bucknell	8	0	1959	1968	1968 (84-69)	
Butler	0	1	1940	1940		1940 (46-37)
Canisius	13	5	1941	**1974**	**1973(96-85)**	**1974(89-81)**
CCNY	0	4	1938	1946		1946 (94-52)
Catholic U.	8	4	1933	1947	1947 (68-33)	1939 (45-40)
Cincinnati	3	5	1948	1962	1953 (86-81)	1962 (64-56)
Clemson					(First Meeting)	
Coast Guard	2	2	1943	1946	1946 (59-46)	1945 (58-44)
Col. of Osteopathy	2	0	1932	1934	1934 (32-13)	
Columbia	1	1	1968	1970	1970 (89-74)	1968 (83-69)
Columbus University	1	0	1942	1942	1942 (47-45)	
Cooper Union	1	0	1933	1933	1933 (33-16)	
Cornell	1	0	1970	1970	1970 (68-56)	
Creighton	3	6	1963	1971	1971 (64-61)	1970 (86-77)
Dartmouth	1	0	1962	1962	1962 (87-60)	
Davis-Elkins	4	0	1935	1942	1942 (44-33)	
Dayton U.	3	1	**1952**	**1962**	**1954(82-58)**	**1962(81-67)**
Delaware	7	1	1931	**1974**	**1974(78-69)**	**1931(33-25)**
DePaul	1	2	1950	1953	1950 (49-41)	1953 (68-62)
Detroit	1	2	1965	1970	1969 (98-96)	1970 (81-77)
Dickinson	2	0	1954	1956	1956 (98-57)	
Drexel	5	1	1945	**1974**	**1974(85-73)**	**1972(77-64)**
Duquesne	11	14	1940	**1974**	**1973(69-67)**	**1974(81-63)**
E. Kentucky	3	0	1952	1970	1970 (84-82)	
E. Michigan	1	0	1973	1973	1973 (93-66)	
Elizabethtown	2	0	1932	1932	1932 (46-14)	
Fairfield	1	0	1972	1972	1972 (108-96)	
Florida State					(First Meeting)	
Fordham	5	1	1954	1962	1962 (60-56)	1956 (84-69)
Furman	2	0	**1954**	**1956**	**1956(73-65)**	
Gallaudet	0	1	1932	1932		1932 (23-17)
Georgetown	15	8	1945	1966	1965 (88-80)	1966 (101-99)
Geo. Washington	1	0	1951	1951	1951 (85-63)	
Georgia	2	0	1970	1970	1970(50-42)	
Georgia Tech	1	1	1949	1971	1949 (67-59)	1971 (70-67)
Geneva	3	0	1938	1952	1952 (103-74)	
Gettysburg	11	2	1946	1968	1968 (96-58)	1962 (57-44)
Haverford College	0	3	1932	1944		1944 (56-42)
Hofstra	5	1	**1969**	**1974**	**1974(66-53)**	**1972(58-56)**
Holy Cross	2	1	1949	1974	1974(94-80)	1972(85-79)
Idaho	1	0	1951	1951	1951 (60-49)	
Houston					(First Meeting)	

48

Opponent	Won	Lost	First Met	Last Met	Last La Salle Victory	Last Opp. Victory
Illinois Wesleyan ..	1	0	1939	1939	1939 (25-23)	....
Indiana	1	1	1957	1969	1969 (108-88)	1957 (93-80)
Iona	2	0	1954	1966	1966 (94-72)	....
Iowa	2	0	1954	1955	1955 (76-73)	....
Kansas	0	1	1952	1952	....	1952 (70-65)
Kentucky	0	2	1954	1955	....	1955 (63-54)
Kutztown	1	1	1945	1945	1945 (64-48)	1945 (54-53)
Lafayette	22	7	1945	1974	1974(87-66)	1973(77-68)
Lock Haven	1	0	1947	1947	1947 (69-36)	....
Lebanon Valley	4	0	1939	1955	1955 (112-70)	....
Lehigh	8	1	1959	1974	1974(87-37)	1972(69-64)
Long Island U.	3	5	1936	1970	1970 (68-53)	1942 (61-37)
Louisville	2	4	1949	1968	1966 (96-92)	1968 (94-71)
Loyola (South)	7	2	1955	1972	1971 (74-53)	1972 (86-80)
Loyola (Md.)	25	1	1934	1954	1954 (97-62)	1944 (53-45)
Manhattan	17	5	1913	1974	1964(75-62)	1974(73-65)
Marshall (W. Va.)	1	2	1943	1970	1970 (76-75)	1970 (97-88)
Massachusetts	1	0	1972	1972	1972 (82-75)	....

```
ALL-TIME INTERSECTIONAL RECORD
          BY CONFERENCE
```

Conference	Won	Lost	Pct.
Southern	11	0	1.000
Yankee	1	0	1.000
Pacific 8	7	1	.875
Big Ten	4	2	.667
Middle Atlantic	162	91	.640
Western Athletic	6	6	.500
Atlantic Coast	9	9	.500
Ivy League	17	18	.486
Ohio Valley	16	15	.531
Southwest	2	2	.500
Mid-American	6	7	.462
Missouri Valley	11	14	.440
Southeast	3	5	.375
Big Eight	1	3	.250
TOTALS	256	173	.598

Opponent	Won	Lost	First Met	Last Met	Last La Salle Victory	Last Opp. Victory
Memphis State U. ..					(First Meeting)	
Miami (Fla.)	9	4	1951	1970	1970 (97-77)	1970 (103-96)
Millersville	19	1	1939	1962	1962 (102-62)	1958 (90-80)
Minnesota	0	1	1966	1966	....	1966 (92-87)
Morehead St.	3	1	1945	1968	1968 (81-73)	1945 (54-47)
Morris-Harvey	3	0	1934	1942	1942 (39-27)	....
Moravian	4	0	1941	1948	1948 (79-58)	....
Mt. St. Mary's	4	4	1931	1939	1939 (34-26)	1933 (21-14)
Muhlenberg	23	8	1941	1963	1963 (88-49)	1959 (92-75)
Murray State	1	0	1952	1952	1952 (105-82)	....
Navy	1	0	1954	1954	1954 (64-48)	....
Nebraska	1	1	1967	1972	1967 (99-76)	1972 (75-60)
Newark	2	0	1942	1943	1943 (50-35)	....
New Mexico State ..	1	0	1973	1973	1973(76-70)	....
N.Y.U.	1	0	1953	1953	1953 (80-63)	....
N. Carolina St.	5	7	1949	1968	1968 (68-63)	1961 (71-68)
North Carolina U. ..	1	0	1947	1947	1947 (65-62)	....
Niagara	15	13	1934	1974	1974(67-65)	1972(71-70)
Northwestern	1	0	1964	1964	1964 (91-69)	....
Notre Dame .	0	3	1972	1974		1974(98-78)

Opponent	Won	Lost	First Met	Last Met	Last La Salle Victory	Last Opp. Victory
Oklahoma A&M	0	1	1940	1940	....	1940 (33-16)
Oklahoma City	1	0	1967	1967	1967 (108-97)	....
Oklahoma U.	0	1	1945	1945		1945 (52-38)
P.M.C.	8	3	1936	1955	1955 (94-39)	1939 (36-31)
Pennsylvania	11	16	1934	1974	1969(78-64)	1974(84-82)
Penn State	2	0	1954	1969	1969 (70-55)	....
Phila. Pharmacy	4	0	1935	1937	1937 (41-15)	....
Phila. Textile	2	0	1931	1932	1932 (31-10)	
Phillips Oilers	0	1	1952	1952		1952 (92-58)
Princeton	2	1	1932	1974	1974(83-78)	1932(25-24)
Providence	1	1	1937	1968	1937 (47-36)	1968 (77-56)
Richmond	4	0	1955	1958	1958 (59-55)	
Rice	0	2	1941	1942		1942 (51-41)
Rider	16	4	1933	1974	1974(84-68)	1971(84-82)
Roanoke	1	1	1937	1939	1937 (32-29)	1939 (31-30)
Rutgers U.	2	0	1961	1974	1974(82-76)	
San Francisco	0	5	1949	1973		1973(74-73)
Santa Clara	1	2	1941	1973	1941(41-37)	1973(71-69)
Scranton	17	9	1932	1960	1960 (82-77)	1952 (55-52)
St. Joseph's	35	37	1901	1974	1969(84-67)	1974(76-71)
St. Bonaventure	1	1	1958	1964	1964 (83-80)	1958 (91-71)
St. Francis (Pa.)	3	0	1947	1969	1969 (107-95)	
St. Francis (N.Y.)	7	2	1937	1948	1948 (53-52)	1943 (47-41)
St. John's (N.Y.)	3	3	1936	1965	1956(85-76)	1965(78-71)
St. Louis	1	4	1951	1963	1954(96-82)	1963(62-61)
Seattle	0	2	1965	1966	....	1966 (84-68)
Seton Hall	12	11	1932	1966	1965 (101-71)	1966 (93-92)
South Carolina	0	1	1969	1969	....	1969 (62-59)
Southern California	3	0	1948	1973	1973(77-72)	....
Stanford	2	0	1953	1974	1974(77-66)	....
Susquehanna	2	0	1946	1947	1947 (47-43)	....
S. W. Missouri State	1	0	1953	1953	1953 (77-70)	
Syracuse	14	10	1955	1974	1970(108-101)	1974(78-65)
Temple	28	34	1900	1974	1974(78-54)	1973(56-54)
Temple Pharmacy	2	1	1931	1932	1932 (33-17)	1931 (32-17)
Tennessee	0	1	1970	1970	....	1970 (55-47)
Texas Tech					(First Meeting)	
Texas Wesleyan	1	0	1948	1948	1948 (69-66)	....
Toledo	1	4	1941	1950	1949 (62-51)	1950 (59-55)
Tulsa	1	2	1940	1972	1971 (63-61)	1972 (80-77)
U.C.L.A.	2	1	1950	1955	1955 (85-77)	1950 (62-57)
Upsala	2	0	1935	1936	1936 (31-24)	....
Ursinus	1	0	1932	1932	1932 (29-26)	
Utah	1	2	1947	1955	1948 (52-46)	1955 (79-69)
Utah State	1	1	1964	1966	1964 (90-85)	1966 (109-97)
Valparaiso	2	0	1957	1958	1958 (97-86)	
Vanderbilt	0	1	1967	1967	....	1967 (100-95)
Villanova	12	13	1934	1974	1974(104-66)	1972(86-73)
Virginia	2	0	1948	1958	1958 (72-64)	....
Wake Forest	1	1	1953	1974	1953(76-59)	1974(95-90)
Washington College	3	0	1940	1942	1942 (60-33)	
West Chester	28	6	1932	1974	1974(73-53)	1940(30-27)
Western Kentucky	9	14	1948	1974	1974(76-65)	1974(85-84)
Westminster	0	1	1938	1938	....	1938 (45-20)
West Virginia	3	0	1955	1968	1968 (100-83)	....
William & Mary	1	0	1949	1949	1949 (63-51)	
Wyoming	0	1	1943	1943	....	1943 (56-32)
Wyomissing P.I.	2	0	1940	1941	1941 (54-41)	....
Xavier (O.)	1	1	1958	1959	1959 (99-80)	1958 (76-65)
Yale	1	0	1970	1970	1970 (81-59)	....
Youngstown	1	1	1952	1953	1953 (94-41)	1952 (68-57)

EXPLORER RESULTS YEAR BY YEAR

(Since World War II)

1944-45 (Won 12, Lost 7)

Opponent	LSC	OPP	Opponent	LSC	OPP
Alumni	58	34	Coast Guard	44	58
Morehead	47	54	Drexel	95	34
Scranton	65	46	Kutztown	64	48
Lafayette	45	52	St. Joseph's	36	39
Kutztown	53	54	Loyola	59	44
Loyola (Md.)	82	42	U.S. Marines	78	53
Atlantic City Hospital	66	64	Drexel	75	46
Atlantic City Navy	37	40	Rider	69	63
Rider	56	45	Oklahoma U.	38	52
Atlantic City Navy	44	52			

1945-46 (Won 9, Lost 14)

Opponent	LSC	OPP	Opponent	LSC	OPP
Alumni	66	43	Catholic U.	54	37
Loyola	45	42	St. Joseph's	38	36
CCNY	52	94	Scranton	41	65
Muhlenberg	33	51	Naval Hospital	69	71
Phila. Navy	48	71	Georgetown	55	53
Coast Guard	59	46	Loyola (Md.)	54	43
Swarthmore	65	40	Gettysburg	54	79
Temple	60	70	Albright	61	67
Lakehurst	58	51	Rider	65	75
Rider	48	74	Manhattan	45	52
Lafayette	49	57	Georgetown	37	54
Albright	59	63			

1946-47 (Won 20, Lost 6)

Opponent	LSC	OPP	Opponent	LSC	OPP
Boston College	76	41	Temple	73	71
Lock Haven	69	36	P.M.C.	95	20
Loyola (Md.)	71	46	Loyola (Md.)	59	49
Seton Hall	42	56	Catholic U.	68	33
Scranton	82	36	St. Joseph's	48	45
Gettysburg	67	48	Georgetown	59	65
Alumni	49	28	Lebanon Valley	72	59
Utah	44	51	Albright	55	47
Muhlenberg	44	59	Seton Hall	54	46
Pennsylvania	56	68	St. Francis (Pa.)	67	55
North Carolina U.	65	62	St. Francis (N.Y.)	53	44
Albright	65	62	*Swarthmore	47	43
Millersville	74	32	*Muhlenberg	41	45

*Middle Atlantic Conference Playoffs

1947-48 (Won 20, Lost 4)

Opponent	LSC	OPP	Opponent	LSC	OPP
Alumni	71	35	Temple	52	54
Millersville	63	47	Texas Wesleyan	69	66
Loyola (Md.)	64	62	Albright	68	30
Moravian	79	58	St. Joseph's	65	70
Arkansas	69	58	Loyola (Md.)	74	58
Lebanon Valley	77	43	St. Francis (N.Y.)	53	52
Southern California	61	48	Pennsylvania	55	43
Utah	52	46	Muhlenberg	74	68
Lafayette	43	39	St. Francis (N.Y.)	59	50
Virginia	67	59	Cincinnati	47	55
Scranton	73	48	Gettysburg	78	62
Georgetown	48	35	*Western Kentucky	60	68

*National Invitation Tourney

1948-49 (Won 21, Lost 7)

Opponent	LSC	OPP	Opponent	LSC	OPP
Lock Haven	67	38	Canisius	59	43
Loyola (Md.)	78	57	Muhlenberg	57	55
Brigham Young	76	54	St. Joseph's	78	41
Millersville	65	52	Bowling Green	45	51
Albright	58	45	Cincinnati	42	36
Georgia Tech	67	59	Manhattan	76	46
Louisville	76	71	Pennsylvania	64	44
San Francisco	45	51	Georgetown	62	45
Muhlenberg	73	56	Lafayette	61	37
Holy Cross	63	61	Manhattan	53	62
Loyola (Md.)	85	61	N. Carolina St.	56	60
Toledo	62	51	Gettysburg	93	60
Baldwin Wallace	49	52	*Cincinnati	49	50
Temple	36	54	*William & Mary	63	51

*Cincinnati Invitation Tourney

1949-50 (Won 21, Lost 4)

Opponent	LSC	OPP	Opponent	LSC	OPP
Millersville	76	41	Temple	67	51
DePaul	49	41	St. Joseph's	79	50
Loyola (Md.)	73	51	Baldwin Wallace	91	65
Temple	60	55	Toledo	55	59
U.C.L.A.	57	62	Loyola (Md.)	71	59
San Francisco	44	46	Muhlenberg	87	60
Georgetown	90	58	Manhattan	65	60
Western Kentucky	80	69	Cincinnati	76	65
Bowling Green	72	62	Gettysburg	61	50
Bloomsburg	67	41	Boston College	83	61
N. Carolina St.	66	51	*Arizona	72	66
Albright	84	37	*Duquesne	47	49
St. Joseph's	74	53			

*National Invitation Tourney

1950-51 (Won 22, Lost 7)

Opponent	LSC	OPP	Opponent	LSC	OPP
Millersville	57	39	N. Carolina St.	74	76
Loyola (Md.)	70	42	Loyola (Md.)	71	42
Albright	58	51	Temple	54	59
St. Joseph's	81	63	Lafayette	71	64
Gettysburg	70	65	Miami (Fla.)	95	84
Niagara	82	56	Miami (Fla.)	75	77
Western Kentucky	63	73	George Washington	85	63
Idaho	60	49	Georgetown	79	74
Temple	82	65	Muhlenberg	69	55
Baldwin Wallace	86	67	Manhattan	64	63
Bowling Green	85	57	Cincinnati	61	62
Duquesne	43	53	Lafayette	66	59
Geneva	87	58	Muhlenberg	83	55
St. Joseph's	77	64	*St. Louis	61	73
Scranton	80	60			

'National Invitation Tourney

1951-52 (Won 25, Lost 7)

Opponent	LSC	OPP	Opponent	LSC	OPP
Loyola (Md.)	93	66	Duquesne	60	71
Niagara	85	74	Youngstown	57	68
Millersville	66	45	Geneva	103	74
West Chester	85	55	Murray State	105	82
Lafayette	62	52	Pennsylvania	75	58
Albright	76	68	St. Joseph's	68	50
Delaware	85	44	Georgetown	68	70
Western Kentucky	67	58	Manhattan	77	55
St. Louis	46	62	Muhlenberg	92	77
Temple	75	59	*Seton Hall	80	76
Eastern Kentucky	77	56	*St. John's	51	45
Scranton	92	55	*Duquesne	59	46
Muhlenberg	95	77	*Dayton	75	64
Loyola (Md.)	91	65	†St. John's	71	62
St. Joseph's	53	54	†Kansas	65	70
Temple	65	50	†Phillips Oilers	58	92

*National Invitation Tourney
†U.S. Olympic Trials

1952-53 (Won 25, Lost 3)

Opponent	LSC	OPP	Opponent	LSC	OPP
Millersville	83	38	Manhattan	63	52
Niagara	87	76	DePaul	62	68
Albright	101	62	St. Joseph's	79	52
West Chester	111	60	Eastern Kentucky	89	67
Dayton	73	64	Loyola (Md.)	73	61
S.W. Missouri St.	77	70	Duquesne	74	66
Arizona	87	68	St. Joseph's	75	63
Stanford	95	80	Temple	57	42
*DePaul	61	63	Muhlenberg	106	73
*Cincinnati	86	81	Georgetown	73	68
*N.Y.U.	80	63	Lafayette	56	50
Wake Forest	76	59	Youngstown	94	41
Loyola (Md.)	89	47	Temple	65	45
Muhlenberg	97	77	†St. John's (N.Y.)	74	75

*Holiday Festival (N.Y.)
†National Invitation Tourney

1953-54 (Won 26, Lost 4)

Opponent	LSC	OPP	Opponent	LSC	OPP
Millersville	79	57	Dayton	82	58
West Chester	65	51	N. Carolina St.	83	78
Albright	78	46	St. Joseph's	73	57
Niagara	66	74	Dickinson	78	51
Lafayette	88	70	Furman	100	83
Georgetown	58	49	Iona	82	69
*U.C.L.A.	62	53	Temple	56	57
*Kentucky	60	73	Fordham	61	56
†St. Louis	77	63	St. Joseph's	78	64
†Niagara	50	69	St. Louis	96	82
†Brigham Young	74	62	‡Fordham (OT)	76	74
Temple	77	63	‡N. Carolina St.	88	81
Loyola (Md.)	97	62	‡Navy	64	48
Muhlenberg	85	65	‡Penn State	69	54
Manhattan	69	61	‡Bradley	92	76

*Kentucky Invitational
†Holiday Festival (N.Y.)
‡NCAA Tourney

1954-55 (Won 26, Lost 5)

Opponent	LSC	OPP	Opponent	LSC	OPP
Millersville	88	72	N. Carolina St.	73	76
Loyola (South)	85	71	St. Joseph's	82	56
P.M.C.	94	39	Georgetown	85	58
Niagara (OT)	76	75	Georgetown	74	46
Lafayette	76	60	Manhattan	76	62
Utah	69	79	Richmond	91	80
*Southern California	49	38	Albright	80	69
*Kentucky	54	63	Muhlenberg	85	71
†Syracuse	103	54	Fordham	64	49
†U.C.L.A.	85	77	Temple (OT)	59	57
†Duquesne	65	67	‡West Virginia	95	61
St. Louis	88	79	‡Princeton	73	46
Brandeis	102	56	‡Canisius	99	64
Muhlenberg	88	79	‡Iowa	76	73
Lebanon Valley	112	70	‡San Francisco	63	77
West Chester	85	50			

*Kentucky Invitational
†Holiday Festival
‡NCAA Tourney

1955-56 (Won 15, Lost 10)

Opponent	LSC	OPP	Opponent	LSC	OPP
Millersville	88	70	Seton Hall	63	64
Muhlenberg	58	69	Richmond	74	59
Albright	96	63	Georgetown (OT)	63	67
Niagara	70	72	Fordham	69	84
Lafayette	95	81	Furman	73	65
Bradley	78	93	Temple	57	60
*San Francisco	62	79	Muhlenberg	81	70
*Syracuse	75	72	Scranton	82	51
*St. John's (N.Y.)	85	76	West Chester	90	78
St. Joseph's	56	69	Villanova	71	64
West Virginia	87	71	Dickinson	98	57
Syracuse	71	64	Villanova	73	76
Pennsylvania	64	52			

*Holiday Festival (N.Y.)

1956-57 (Won 17, Lost 9)

Opponent	LSC	OPP	Opponent	LSC	OPP
Millersville	61	53	West Chester	57	51
Albright	75	52	Syracuse	82	94
Lafayette	75	84	Pennsylvania	84	73
Bradley	87	77	Muhlenberg	68	93
Niagara	83	74	Georgetown	62	75
Indiana	80	93	Seton Hall	61	70
N. Carolina St.	83	78	Temple	63	61
*Western Kentucky	76	89	Duquesne	87	80
*Seton Hall	82	72	Muhlenberg	99	82
*Valparaiso	103	73	Richmond	60	52
Manhattan	81	72	Fordham	84	66
St. Joseph's	85	97	Villanova	75	61
Cincinnati	58	74	St. Joseph's	61	57

*Orange Bowl Classic (Miami)

1957-58 (Won 16, Lost 9)

Opponent	LSC	OPP	Opponent	LSC	OPP
Millersville	80	90	Valparaiso	97	86
Albright	83	55	Xavier (Ohio)	65	76
Lafayette	82	74	Muhlenberg	82	80
Manhattan	72	59	St. Bonaventure	71	91
Pennsylvania	66	67	Temple	61	71
Niagara (OT)	69	68	West Chester	68	66
*Virginia	72	64	Scranton	86	60
*Richmond (OT)	59	55	N. Carolina St.	62	71
Syracuse (OT)	59	55	St. Joseph's	77	82
Muhlenberg	67	61	Morehead St.	89	86
Villanova (OT)	111	105	Seton Hall	80	79
Duquesne	55	74	Villanova	75	64
Georgetown	62	64			

*Richmond (Va.) Invitational

1958-59 (Won 16, Lost 7)

Opponent	LSC	OPP	Opponent	LSC	OPP
Millersville	85	58	Western Kentucky	74	96
Niagara	56	72	Pennsylvania	70	73
Lafayette	84	77	Muhlenberg	75	92
Lehigh	81	47	Seton Hall	83	69
N. Carolina St.	67	82	Georgetown	102	72
Western Kentucky	84	75	Duquesne	72	65
Manhattan	78	71	Albright	93	62
Bucknell	70	68	St. Joseph's	63	70
Muhlenberg	92	77	West Chester	85	67
Syracuse	79	71	Xavier (Ohio)	99	80
Temple	67	64	Villanova	57	63
Canisius	77	64			

1959-60 (Won 16, Lost 6)

Opponent	LSC	OPP	Opponent	LSC	OPP
Millersville	76	60	Western Kentucky	70	76
Bucknell	84	62	West Chester	85	68
Lehigh	86	54	St. Joseph's	80	73
Manhattan	71	58	Albright	73	67
Lafayette	81	73	Muhlenberg	86	63
Niagara	64	48	Pennsylvania	62	66
Canisius	82	68	Temple	53	77
Duquesne	68	65	Muhlenberg	91	59
Morehead State	63	58	N. Carolina St.	65	80
Syracuse (OT)	84	90	Scranton	82	77
Georgetown	80	79	Villanova	52	68

1960-61 (Won 15, Lost 7)

Opponent	LSC	OPP	Opponent	LSC	OPP
Millersville	82	48	West Chester	83	67
Albright	65	62	Temple	57	63
Rutgers	85	63	Western Kentucky	69	73
Niagara	71	77	St. Joseph's	54	65
Bucknell	79	69	Gettysburg	67	62
Muhlenberg	84	67	Muhlenberg	81	64
N. Carolina St.	68	71	Syracuse	81	75
Miami (Fla.)	88	74	Lafayette	104	86
Lehigh	77	62	Canisius	73	94
Manhattan	74	68	Villanova	76	71
Pennsylvania	67	63	Duquesne	63	78

1961-62 (Won 16, Lost 9)

Opponent	LSC	OPP	Opponent	LSC	OPP
Millersville	102	62	Duquesne	66	80
Albright	78	69	Temple	51	64
Niagara	64	78	Bucknell	91	78
Lehigh	71	59	Fordham	60	56
Pennsylvania	69	57	Delaware	69	68
*Dartmouth	87	60	Canisius	73	63
*Cincinnati	56	64	St. Joseph's	72	71
*Dayton	67	81	Lafayette	69	73
Manhattan	76	69	Villanova	63	65
Muhlenberg	90	51	Georgetown	78	76
Syracuse	69	53	Western Kentucky	88	84
Gettysburg	44	57	Villanova	67	75
Miami (Fla.)	73	61			

*Holiday Festival (N.Y.)

1962-63 (Won 16, Lost 8)

Opponent	LSC	OPP	Opponent	LSC	OPP
Creighton	72	91	Seton Hall	89	80
Lafayette	95	59	Delaware	64	62
Niagara	76	79	Temple	81	71
Lehigh	85	34	Gettysburg	80	65
Albright	67	57	Syracuse	74	66
Bucknell	105	55	Pennsylvania	74	78
*Brigham Young	73	84	Canisius	53	76
*Delaware	80	64	Duquesne	73	69
*Bowling Green	74	67	St. Joseph's	49	66
Miami (Fla.)	78	76	Georgetown	75	72
Muhlenberg	88	49	Villanova	47	63
Manhattan	78	61	†St. Louis	61	62

*Quaker City Tourney
†National Invitation Tourney

1963-64 (Won 16, Lost 9)

Opponent	LSC	OPP	Opponent	LSC	OPP
Albright	76	44	Miami (Fla.)	99	121
Creighton	62	77	Georgetown	81	85
Louisville	60	70	Gettysburg	50	46
Bucknell	93	75	St. Joseph's	80	70
Lehigh	68	40	Manhattan	75	62
Niagara	58	54	Villanova	63	59
*Northwestern	91	69	Seton Hall	68	75
*Georgetown	80	69	Temple	57	63
*St. Bonaventure	83	80	Canisius	91	81
Pennsylvania	61	58	Western Kentucky	95	107
Lafayette	100	86	Utah State	90	85
Syracuse	63	61	Loyola (South)	61	63
Duquesne	58	89			

*Quaker City Tourney

1964-65 (Won 15, Lost 8)

Opponent	LSC	OPP	Opponent	LSC	OPP
Albright	81	57	Pennsylvania	78	64
Delaware	97	47	*St. John's	71	78
Miami (Fla.)	90	86	*Temple	83	70
Niagara	67	59	*Syracuse	73	70
Seattle	74	76	Louisville	80	92

1964-65 (Continued)

	LSC	OPP		LSC	OPP
Villanova	72	86	Creighton	66	84
Duquesne	83	69	Western Kentucky	91	77
Syracuse	81	104	Seton Hall	101	71
Lafayette	91	73	Georgetown	88	80
Loyola (South)	72	69	St. Joseph's	85	93
Temple	81	74	†Detroit	86	93
Gettysburg	91	68			

*Holiday Festival (N.Y.)
†National Invitation Tourney

1965-66 (Won 10, Lost 15)

Opponent	LSC	OPP	Opponent	LSC	OPP
Albright	97	73	Creighton	90	104
Western Kentucky	67	93	Utah State	97	109
Seton Hall	92	93	Seattle	68	84
Georgetown	99	101	American U.	103	93
Bucknell	87	68	Lafayette	81	93
Niagara	87	88	Villanova	78	70
*Brigham Young	71	69	Gettysburg	99	76
*Temple	59	66	Temple	86	85
*Minnesota	87	92	Iona	94	72
St. Joseph's	69	92	Canisius	95	81
Pennsylvania	76	90	Louisville	96	92
Syracuse	85	98	Miami (Fla.)	102	108
Duquesne	77	70			

*Quaker City Tourney

1966-67 (Won 14, Lost 12)

Opponent	LSC	OPP	Opponent	LSC	OPP
Gettysburg	103	67	Syracuse	81	102
Miami (Fla.)	99	82	W. Kentucky	86	95
Niagara	69	72	Creighton (OT)	88	83
Albright	84	50	Loyola (South)	125	80
*Nebraska	99	76	Temple	65	79
*Vanderbilt	95	100	Oklahoma City	108	97
Pennsylvania	85	83	Duquesne	77	66
Louisville	88	106	Villanova	59	68
†Syracuse	84	88	Canisius	75	93
†Niagara	86	72	St. Joseph's	85	96
†Bowling Green	78	77	Lafayette	85	72
St. Francis (Pa.)	84	74	‡St. Joseph's	73	70
American U. (OT)	90	94	‡Temple	61	78

*Vanderbilt Tourney (2nd Place)
†Quaker City Tourney (5th Place)
‡Middle Atlantic Conference (2nd Place)

1967-68 (Won 20, Lost 8)

Opponent	LSC	OPP	Opponent	LSC	OPP
Rider	59	50	Loyola (La.)	71	51
Gettysburg	96	58	Syracuse	105	81
Albright	82	40	Western Kentucky	79	84
Bucknell	84	69	Pennsylvania	45	57
Niagara	83	100	Morehead State	81	73
*Providence	56	77	‡American U.	84	57
*N. Carolina St.	68	63	‡Temple	87	69
†Louisville	71	94	§Columbia	69	83
†West Virginia	100	83	Duquesne (OT)	80	79
†Syracuse	78	68	Creighton	71	77
Miami (Fla.)	92	84	West Chester	79	55
St. Joseph's	103	71	Lafayette	74	45

1967-68 (Won 20, Lost 8)

Opponent	LSC	OPP	Opponent	LSC	OPP
Rider	59	50	Western Kentucky	79	84
Gettysburg	96	58	Pennsylvania	45	57
Albright	82	40	Duquesne (OT)	80	79
Bucknell	84	69	Creighton	71	77
Niagara	83	100	West Chester	79	55
*Providence	56	77	Lafayette	74	45
*N. Carolina St.	68	63	Temple	64	60
†Louisville	71	94	American U.	74	65
†West Virginia	100	83	Canisius	80	64
†Syracuse	78	68	Villanova	56	64
Miami (Fla.)	92	84	Morehead State	81	73
St. Joseph's	103	71	‡American U.	84	57
Loyola (La.)	71	51	‡Temple	87	69
Syracuse	105	81	§Columbia	69	83

*Boston Garden Tourney (3rd Place)
§NCAA Tourney (Eliminated)
†Holiday Festival, N.Y. (5th Place)
‡Middle Atlantic Conference Playoffs (1st Place)

1968-69 (Won 23, Lost 1)

Opponent	LSC	OPP	Opponent	LSC	OPP
Baltimore	100	57	Western Kentucky	88	81
Rider	79	59	Pennsylvania	78	64
Miami (Fla.)	96	71	Temple	101	85
Niagara	88	73	St. Francis (Pa.)	107	95
Canisius	68	56	Loyola (N.O.)	102	65
Albright	91	65	Lafayette	97	65
*Penn State	70	55	Villanova	74	67
*Indiana	108	88	American U.	96	72
*South Carolina	59	62	St. Joseph's	84	67
Hofstra	89	68	Duquesne	85	71
Creighton	103	84	Detroit	98	96
Syracuse	83	63	West Chester	91	73

*ECAC Quaker City Tournament (2nd Place)

1969-70 (Won 14, Lost 12)

Opponent	LSC	OPP	Opponent	LSC	OPP
Hofstra	83	64	Western Kentucky	80	102
Albright	95	59	Loyola (South)	85	79
Eastern Kentucky	84	82	Creighton	77	86
Marshall	88	97	Duquesne	64	67
West Chester	92	80	Pennsylvania	67	76
*Yale	81	59	Canisius	70	80
*Tennessee	47	55	Lafayette	102	73
†Georgia	76	66	Detroit	77	81
†Cornell	68	56	American U.	106	86
‡Columbia	89	74	Niagara	101	90
St. Joseph's (2 OT)	99	101	Miami (Fla.)	96	103
Syracuse	108	101	Villanova	85	96
Temple	61	69	Rider	72	66

*Volunteer Classic, Knoxville, Tenn.
†Quaker City Tournament, Philadelphia

1970-71 (Won 20, Lost 7)

Opponent	LSC	OPP	Opponent	LSC	OPP
Albright	89	59	Drexel	81	63
Long Island	68	53	Hofstra	79	62
Miami	97	77	Loyola (N.O.)	74	53
Marshall	76	75	Syracuse	68	75
W. Chester	82	68	Canisius	92	55
Penn	88	107	Villanova	73	69
*Georgia	50	42	Duquesne	86	95
*Boston College	75	63	Creighton	64	61
Tulsa	63	61	American	62	54
Temple	63	58	St. Joseph's	56	66
W. Kentucky	91	76	Rider (OT)	82	84
Niagara	96	79	†Lafayette	74	71
Lafayette	93	82	†St. Joseph's (OT)	76	81
			‡Georgia Tech	67	70

*Charlotte Invitational
†Middle Atlantic Conference Playoffs
‡National Invitational Tourney

1971-72 (Won 6, Lost 19)

Opponent	LSC	OPP	Opponent	LSC	OPP
Lehigh (H)	64	69-	W. Kentucky (A)	84	103-
Hofstra (A)	56	58-	Loyola (South) (A)	80	86-
Niagara (H)	70	71-	American (H)	59	53
Tulsa (H)	77	80-	Penn (H)	66	80-
West Chester (A)	86	62	Canisius (A)	80	78
*Baylor	81	68	Temple (H)	56	67-
*Nebraska	60	75-	Notre Dame (H)	71	97-
†Boston College	61	62-	Drexel (A)	64	77-
†Fairfield	108	96	Holy Cross (A)	79	85-
†Massachusetts	82	75	Biscayne (A)	93	103-
St. Joseph's (H)	55	72-	Duquesne (A)	69	81-
Lafayette (H)	66	86-	Syracuse (H)	80	87-
			Villanova (H)	73	86-

*Cornhusker Classic, Lincoln, Neb.
†Quaker City Tournament

1972-73 (Won 15, Lost 10)

Opponent	LSC	OPP	Opponent	LSC	OPP
Lehigh (A)	75	59	Lafayette (A)	68	77-
Army (H)	73	63	Niagara (A)	80	72
Biscayne (H)	69	67	Pennsylvania (H)	45	57-
*USF	73	74-	Duquesne (H)	69	67
*Santa Clara (OT)	69	71-	Western Kentucky	108	80
E. Michigan (H)	93	66	Syracuse (A)	84	91-
W. Chester (H)	92	52	Canisius (H)	96	85
†U. of S. California	77	72	Notre Dame (A)	71	87-
†New Mexico State	76	70	Drexel (A)	72	57
†St. Joseph's	52	77-	Temple (H)	54	56-
St. Joseph's (H)	55	68-	American (A)	79	88-
Rider (H)	78	67	Villanova (H)	101	79
Hofstra (H)	76	55			

*Cable Car Classic (Oakland, Cal.)
†Quaker City Tourney (Philadelphia, Pa.)

(1973-74 RESULTS ON PAGE 40)

Brother Daniel Burke,
F.S.C., Ph.D.
President, La Salle College

THE LA SALLE STORY

La Salle College, now in its 111th year of service to higher education and the Philadelphia Community, was founded March 20, 1863 by the Brothers of the Christian Schools and derives its name from the founder of the Christian Brothers, St. John Baptist de La Salle.

In 1929, having outgrown three previous Philadelphia locations, the campus was moved to its present site at 20th and Olney Avenue in the East Germantown section of the city.

Since 1945, La Salle has experienced dramatic growth. Before the closing days of the war, the college had an enrollment of less than 500 attending classes in plant facilities valued at only $1.5 million. Today, 6300 day and evening division students attend classes on La Salle's 40-acre campus, appraised at $30 million.

Olney Hall, a $4.4 million, 100,000-square-foot complex opened in September, 1971, contains 39 classrooms, 15 student seminar and study rooms, and 107 faculty offices as well as such special-purpose areas as a planetarium, an amphitheatre, language laboratories and audio-visual rooms. It houses the liberal arts area departments of English, Education, History, Languages, Political Science and Sociology.

HAYMAN HALL

Hayman Hall, the college's new $4 million physical recreation center which opened this past September, contains the Joseph Kirk Memorial Natatorium with separate swimming and diving facilities, an underwater observation deck, and seats for 1700 spectators. Three regulation-size basketball courts, a one-twelfth mile indoor suspended track, and areas for fencing, wrestling, squash, handball, gymnastics and general exercise are the other features of the complex.

Ten modern residence halls accommodate 800 out-of-town students. A $2 million, three-story College Union Building, completed in 1959, includes a Little Theatre as well as dining halls, assembly rooms, ballroom and other student facilities.

The $2.5 million Holroyd Science Center, opened in 1960, houses lecture rooms and laboratories for study and research in Biology, Chemistry, Geology, Physics and Psychology. The David Leo Lawrence Memorial Library, built in 1952, contains 175,000 volumes and periodical files for some 700 journals, and a library annex in the former Wister Hall gymnasium opened last year, increasing library space by 50%.

The Army ROTC program, initiated in 1950, is available to freshmen, who may apply for ROTC scholarships for advance studies.

La Salle's day and evening divisions offer degree programs in Arts and Sciences and Business Administration. The 350-member faculty is composed of Christian Brothers, priests and lay professors. The college has been co-educational in the evening division since February, 1967 and in its day school since September, 1970.

Students at La Salle come from some 200 public and private schools in 21 States, most of them located in the northeastern part of the United States. Fourteen countries are also represented in the student body. Over 75 per cent of them plan graduate work and about 1,000 degrees are conferred annually on day and evening division seniors. La Salle's alumni totals 16,000 with more than 80 per cent of them still living and working in the tri-state area of Pennsylvania, New Jersey and Delaware.